ANTON CHEKHOV

ANTON CHEKHOV

A Brother's Memoir

MIKHAIL CHEKHOV

Translated by Eugene Alper

palgrave
macmillan

ANTON CHEKHOV
English-language translation copyright © 2010 by Eugene Alper.
All rights reserved.

Frontispiece, p. ii: Chekhov family and friends in front of Sadovaya-Kudrinskaya home, 1890. (*Top row, left to right*) Ivan, Alexander, Father; (*second row*) unknown friend, Lika Mizinova, Masha, Mother, Seriozha Kiseliov; (*bottom row*) Mikhail, Anton.

First published in 1933 in the Soviet Union as *Vokrug Chekhova: Vstrechi i vpechatlenia.*

First published in English in 2010 by PALGRAVE MACMILLAN® in the United States—a division of St. Martin's Press LLC, 175 Fifth Avenue, New York, NY 10010.

Where this book is distributed in the UK, Europe and the rest of the world, this is by Palgrave Macmillan, a division of Macmillan Publishers Limited, registered in England, company number 785998, of Houndmills, Basingstoke, Hampshire RG21 6XS.

Palgrave Macmillan is the global academic imprint of the above companies and has companies and representatives throughout the world.

Palgrave® and Macmillan® are registered trademarks in the United States, the United Kingdom, Europe and other countries.

ISBN: 978-0-230-61883-1

Library of Congress Cataloging-in-Publication Data
Chekhov, Mikhail Pavlovich, 1865–1936.
    [Vokrug Chekhova. English]
    Anton Chekhov : a brother's memoir / Mikhail Chekhov ; translated by Eugene Alper.
      p. cm.
    Originally published in the Soviet Union in 1933 as Vokrug Chekhova.
    Summary: "In a style reminiscent of Anton Chekhov himself—realistic, intimate, and dynamic—Mikhail Chekhov shares unparalleled memories and insights, transporting readers into the world of the Chekhov family. He visits the places where his brother lived and worked and introduces the people he knew and loved, Leo Tolstoy and Piotr Tchaikovsky among them. As a unique eyewitness to the beloved writer's formative years and his artistic maturity, Mikhail Chekhov shows here first-hand the events that inspired the plots for The Seagull, The Black Monk, and The Steppe, among other enduring works. Captivating, surprising, and a joy to read, this memoir reveals the remarkable life of one the most masterful storytellers of our time"—Provided by publisher.
    ISBN 978-0-230-61883-1 (hardback)
    1. Chekhov, Anton Pavlovich, 1860–1904.   2. Chekhov, Anton Pavlovich, 1860–1904—Family.   3. Authors, Russian—19th century—Biography.   I. Alper, Eugene. II. Title.
PG3458.C4613 2010
891.72'3—dc22
[B]

        2009036132

A catalogue record of the book is available from the British Library.

Design by Letra Libre, Inc.

First edition: January 2010
10 9 8 7 6 5 4 3 2
Printed in the United States of America.

CONTENTS

TRANSLATOR'S NOTE AND ACKNOWLEDGMENTS

Russian names are notorious for their length and difficulty, so an explanation may be in order. In Russian, it is common to address adults with their full first name plus their patronym (the name of their father). Thus, the author of this book is Mikhail (first name) Pavlovich (patronym) Chekhov (last name). As people become more intimate with one another, they begin addressing each other by their first name, often in its shortened or endearing version. Thus Mikhail Pavlovich becomes simply "Mikhail" or "Misha" or "Mishka" or "Mishenka." Or, in another example, Tatiana Lvovna becomes "Tatiana" or "Tania" or "Tanechka." Here is a short guide to other names and their modifications as they appear in the book.

Anton Pavlovich = Anton = Antosha
Aleksey = Aliosha = Alioshka
Alexander = Sasha

Evgenia Yakovlevna = Evgenia = Evochka
Ivan = Vanya = Vanyusha
Maria Pavlovna = Maria = Masha
Maria Dorimedontovna = Mariushka
Nikolay = Kolia

A note by the author in chapter 2 is set as a footnote; all other notes are by me and presented as numbered endnotes. In the notes, Chekhov's stories, books, and plays are provided with the year of their first publication or performance. Since the titles of the stories can be, and have been, translated differently, the notes also contain their Russian names transliterated in English.

Russian measures of length—*versta* and kilometer—have been converted to miles.

In chronological order, my first thank you goes to the one whose name is unknown to us but who lit the fire. Then, to my mother. Then to Professor Michael Finke, now at the University of Illinois at Urbana-Champaign, for giving me the idea of looking into the Chekhov brothers' memoirs and for his generous advice thereafter. Next I thank my friend Yellena Orloff for being the first and pickiest reader: your thoroughness and humor spur me to a different level. Thanks to Maria-Gracia Inglessis for quiet but continuous support. Finally, I dedicate this work of translation to Sophia, in hope that someday, maybe, the speaking of the same language may return.

PREFACE

*A*nton Chekhov: A Brother's Memoir was originally published in the Soviet Union in 1933 as *Vokrug Chekhova: Vstrechi i vpechatlenia* [*Around Chekhov: Encounters and Impressions*]. Mikhail Chekhov was sixty-eight at the time of publication and was living in his famous brother's house in Yalta, with his seventy-year old sister.

Born in 1865, Mikhail was the youngest child in the Chekhov family. His parents, Pavel and Evgenia, already had five children: Alexander, Nikolay, Anton, Ivan, and Maria. The family lived in Taganrog, a thriving town of 25,000 residents on the Sea of Azov in southern Russia.

In 1875 Alexander and Nikolay went to Moscow to attend school; their father later joined them as he fled Taganrog to avoid debtor's prison. A few months later their mother arrived with the two youngest children, Maria and Mikhail, who was ten years old. Finally, the middle brothers Ivan and Anton arrived in Moscow in 1877 and 1879 respectively.

After finishing school, Mikhail enrolled in Moscow University. He graduated from law school but did not pursue a legal career. Initially, he made a living working for the government and eventually supervised a provincial treasury department.

In 1901, he resigned from the government and moved to Saint Petersburg to work for Aleksey Suvorin, Anton's close friend and occasional publisher. After his time in publishing, he became a teacher. Throughout his life, however, Mikhail wrote short stories, novels, poetry, plays, and translations.

Much like his older brother Anton, Mikhail began writing at a young age. He published children's stories while still a university student, and his first book-length translation from English to Russian appeared when he was only twenty-six. Later, living in Yaroslavl—a city with a rich theatrical life—Mikhail wrote theater reviews for the local press and a prestigious Saint Petersburg magazine, *Theater and Art*. In Saint Petersburg, he published *Essays and Stories* and the novel *Bluestocking* in 1904, and another novel, *Orphans,* in 1905. The second edition of *Essays and Short Stories,* published in 1907, brought Mikhail an Honorable Mention from the Literary Section of the Academy of Sciences. In 1910, he authored another collection of stories entitled *Reed-Pipe.* From 1907 to 1917, he published and edited *Golden Childhood,* a biweekly magazine for children. Mikhail also wrote several hundred stories, novellas, essays, and poems for the magazine under different names. After the Bolshevik revolution in 1917 and throughout the 1920s, Mikhail contributed to various children's magazines and published several books of children's stories under the pen names "K. Treplev" and "S. Vershinin," names of characters from Anton's plays. He continued his translation work during that period and published ten translations of English and French books. In 1926, he wrote the play *Duel,* based on Anton's novel, as well as an original movie script.

Mikhail's role as Anton's biographer began in 1905 when, on the first anniversary of his brother's death, he was asked to share his recollections in an essay for a Moscow publication, *The Monthly Magazine for Everyone.* In 1906, the essay was reprinted in a book called *To the Memory of A. P. Chekhov.* Mikhail published a second essay of recollections the same year, and a third in 1907. In 1912, his sister Maria published a collection of Anton's letters and Mikhail wrote a biographical preface for it.

Mikhail wrote his first biographical book, *Anton Chekhov and His Plots,* in 1923. He went on to publish *Anton Chekhov, the Theater, Actors and "Tatiana Repina"* (1924), *Anton Chekhov on Vacation* (1929), and a commentary to a volume of Anton's previously unpublished letters (1930). Finally, in 1929, Mikhail finished writing the book you are now holding. This book represents a compilation of the most important stories from Mikhail's previously published recollections, as well as valuable new material. First published in 1933, the book was reprinted in the Soviet Union at least five more times.[1]

From the beginning, Mikhail's recollections have been relied on heavily by Anton Chekhov biographers. They have been referenced in the works of Constance Garnett (1920), David Magarshak (1952), Ernest Simmons (1962), Ronald Hingley (1976), Donald Rayfield (1997), and Philip Callow (1998), to name a few. This is the first translation of Mikhail's book into English.

In 1936, Mikhail wrote to his son,

Often and for a long time, especially in the mornings, when everyone in the house is still asleep, I feel so inspired that I begin planning to write one book or another. . . . You're right: fate ruled it so that I, and only I, could and should have written books and commentaries about Anton. . . . How many times I began work on most pressing topics about him! For example, about his mysterious relationship with Suvorin (for no one really knows its main drivers!) . . . But my muse is no longer what it used to be! I have fulfilled what I was meant to fulfill and it's time for me to get into the box. . . . Enough! Now you write, my dear, you publish, you tilt at windmills. And as for me, I will take to my grave masses of unpublished, unused materials about Chekhov![2]

In November of that year, Mikhail died from coronary disease at age seventy-one.

—*Eugene Alper*

CHRONOLOGY

October 6, 1865	Mikhail's birth in Taganrog.
1875–1876	The Chekhovs move to Moscow.
1879	Anton joins the family and enrolls as a student at the Moscow University School of Medicine.
1880	Anton's first story appears in *Dragonfly* magazine.
1884	Anton graduates; publishes his first book, *The Tales of Melpomene*.
1885	Mikhail becomes a student in the Moscow University Law School.
1887	Anton's first play *Ivanov* opens in Moscow. Mikhail publishes his first stories in various children's magazines.
1888	Anton publishes the novella *Steppe* and the book *Short Stories*. He receives the Pushkin Award from the Academy of Sciences for the second edition of *In the Twilight*.
1890	Anton travels to the Sakhalin Island in the North Pacific. Mikhail graduates

and begins his first appointment as tax inspector in Efremov, 200 miles south of Moscow. Later in the year he transfers to Aleksin, 100 miles south of Moscow.

1891   Mikhail does translations for *Foreign Literature* magazine.

1892   Anton, Maria, and their parents move to Melikhovo, the estate purchased by Anton, 45 miles south of Moscow. Several months later Mikhail moves to the Melikhovo estate with the family.

1893   Mikhail publishes *Dictionary of Farming*.

1894   Mikhail is transferred to Uglich, 150 miles north of Moscow, and later promoted to collegiate secretary. Anton travels to Vienna, Trieste, Naples, Venice, Milan, Genoa, Nice, and Paris.

1896   Mikhail marries Olga Vladykina (1871–1950).

1897   Mikhail transfers to Yaroslavl, is promoted to titular counselor, and begins to write columns and theater reviews for various publications.

1898   Mikhail and Olga give birth to their daughter Evgenia. Pavel Chekhov dies. Anton buys a parcel of land, 930 miles

	south of Moscow near Yalta, and begins building a house.
1899	Melikhovo estate sold; Anton and Maria move their mother to Yalta.
1901	Mikhail and Olga's son Sergey is born. Mikhail resigns from government work, accepts Aleksey Suvorin's offer to work for *New Time,* and moves to Saint Petersburg. Anton marries Olga Knipper (1868–1959).
1904	Anton dies from consumption. Mikhail publishes book *Essays and Stories.*
1905	Mikhail publishes his first recollections of Anton in *The Monthly Magazine for Everyone.*
1907	Mikhail publishes the biweekly *Golden Childhood* (until 1917); begins teaching in two private schools in Saint Petersburg. The second edition of *Essays and Stories* receives an Honorable Mention from the Academy of Science.
1912	A two-volume set of Anton's letters are published with Mikhail's biographical essay.
1919	Evgenia Chekhov dies in Yalta. Maria becomes the life-long caretaker of Anton's house in Yalta .

1922	Mikhail and family move to Moscow. After registering for unemployment, Mikhail finds work in the central warehouse of the State Publishing House.
1923	Mikhail publishes *Anton Chekhov and His Plots* and continues his translation work.
1926	Mikhail joins his sister Maria in Yalta.
1933	*Around Chekhov: Encounters and Impressions* is published in Moscow.
November 14, 1936	Mikhail dies in Yalta.

ANTON CHEKHOV

I

OUR
ANCESTRY

MANY PEOPLE CONSIDERED OUR UNCLE MITROFAN Egorovich[1] to be peculiar, eccentric—God's fool even. But there were others, like my brother, the writer Anton Chekhov, who treated him with affection and respect. Uncle Mitrofan dedicated his life to charity. He served as a council member and churchwarden, and helped found the Taganrog Charitable Society, created for the relief of the poor. His house was always open to those less fortunate, and on his birthday he would set up tables full of food in the courtyard and open his gates for everyone to come eat.

Mitrofan was a religious man who hosted collective prayers at his house. But he also loved to attend the theater and heartily enjoyed comedies and vaudevilles like *Mama's Boy* or *Misfortunes of a Gentle Heart*.[2] He dressed elegantly in a top hat, and his house appeared to be full of prosperity. His days began at dawn and ended late at night.

He only rested on Sundays, when he would spend the entire day reading and talking with his children.[3] He adored his children and would address them respectfully, as if they were adults, and treat them with such affection that we his nephews were often jealous. When we staged plays at home with Anton, Uncle Mitrofan would be our guest of honor and our main critic. He certainly had a literary gift; his letters were impeccable in their style and poetic quality. He was deeply romantic in his youth, and it showed in his writing.[4] Our family kept a carefully bound book of the letters he wrote to my parents during his travels around Russia before his marriage in 1859. I am convinced that Uncle Mitrofan's literary gift rubbed off on us, especially to my brothers Anton and Alexander, who both became professional writers.

Mitrofan Egorovich's love and marriage is an interesting story. There was a man who worked in the office of Taganrog's governor. His name was Evtushevsky, and he had a daughter named Lyudmila, who went by the diminutive Milechka. She bore a striking resemblance to Maximiliana, the daughter of the Duke of Gessen Darmstadt, who had married crown heir Alexander Nikolaevich and taken the name of Maria Alexanderovna. Mitrofan Egorovich, having seen a portrait of Maximiliana in some publication, fell in love with the princess at first sight and transferred this affection to Milechka. He proposed to her but she refused, and our hopelessly romantic Uncle disappeared from the city without a word to any of us. Eventually however, letters from his travels began to arrive.

At the time, traveling was very difficult; in fact, the 290 miles between Taganrog and Kharkov boasted not a single town. You rarely met anyone on the road, save perhaps peasants on carts, and one had to sleep in the open in the middle of a vast steppe. These were the "new places" described so well in Grigory Danilevsky's novel of the same title.[5] They were characterized by uninhabited expanses and highway robbers, and conjured up folktales about mysterious adventures with demons and mean spirits. When our Father, Pavel Egorovich,[6] had to travel to Kharkov to pick up goods our family would pray for his safe return. Nikolaevsky, the only existing railroad line, was still under construction, and the hundred-mile journey from Moscow to Tver took one and a half days, but it was nevertheless the best travel option in terms of speed and convenience.

Uncle Mitrofan wrote deeply engaging letters about his journey. He described his visits to Moscow and Saint Petersburg and his impressions of the first railroad in a romantic style. But it was his letter about visiting Tsarskoe Selo[7] that was read over and over, and that revealed the secret purpose of his trip.

Uncle had gone to the garden at the Royal Palace hoping to steal a glance at the woman who so closely resembled his beloved. To his surprise, he did indeed spot Tsar Alexander II himself and his wife, the former Princess Maximiliana, walking toward him! Uncle Mitrofan kneeled as they approached, so Alexander II, thinking he was a supplicant, stopped and asked him, "What is it that you want?" Mitrofan replied, "I don't want anything, sire. I am only happy that I have seen the woman that my beloved resembles so much." Maria Alexanderovna probably did not even understand his words, but Alexander bade my Uncle to stand, patted him on the back, and walked away.

The story is, of course, very simple. But at that time, especially to those of us living in a remote region deep in Russia's south, it sounded impressive. It was also thanks to this story that Milechka agreed to marry Uncle Mitrofan Egorovich when he returned. He probably embellished the anecdote of the royal encounter, but that was just how our romantic Uncle wrote.

And so Mitrofan and Milechka lived together into old age, and always made us feel welcome in their cozy little house. Later, when we lived in the north and only occasionally visited Taganrog, we always liked staying at Uncle Mitrofan's house. It was there that Anton picked up certain details that later appeared in "The Marshal's Widow" and other stories.

I always suspected that Uncle Mitrofan wrote more than just letters. When I was twenty-five, I began receiving letters from him, enclosing pages of excerpts from some creative descriptions of nature all about "wildflowers behind the monastery walls on monks' graves," "little creeks" playfully running among "a dewy meadow," and so on. It was easy to guess from their manner and style that he was the author of these excerpts.

As I mentioned, Uncle Mitrofan was the churchwarden and, both because of this post and his personality, he enjoyed entertaining members of the clergy at home. One of his favorite guests was archpriest F. P. Pokrovsky. Very handsome and worldly, he liked brandishing his erudition as well as sporting his smart cassock. He possessed a deep and powerful baritone, and in his youth had dreamed of becoming an opera singer. Unable to develop his gift as a professional, he had had to settle for being archpriest of the Taganrog Cathedral. However, even there he conducted himself like a true artist, theatrically officiating the mass and singing so forcefully that his booming voice would overpower the choir and resonate in all corners of the vast cathedral. Listening to him was indeed like being at the opera.

Pokrovsky also taught theology at the local school that all my brothers and I attended. But in class Pokrovsky strangely lost all of his stage presence, to the point that he didn't ask any questions. He would read a newspaper during class, then call a pupil to the front of the room, and automatically give him a C without even listening to him.

Pokrovsky transferred his disapproval of our Father's religious formalism onto us. When he was older, Anton more than once related a remark that Pokrovsky had made to our Mother in his presence: "Nothing good will come of your children, Evgenia Yakovlevna, nothing good. Except maybe your eldest, Alexander." He liked giving his students mocking nicknames, too; in fact, he was the first to call Anton *Antosha Chekhonte,* which later became my brother's pen name.

Anton Chekhov exhibited a peculiar attachment to Pokrovsky, as evidenced by the following anecdote. By 1887 relations between Russia and Bulgaria had entered a surreal stage. After independence, the Bulgarians unexpectedly elected Ferdinand Coburg as their royal prince. The Russian autocracy, which still felt proprietary toward Bulgaria, felt insulted by the bold and insolent actions of this "rescued Slavic people." Ferdinand attained normalcy with Russia only after much effort. In celebration, and hoping to improve public opinion, Bulgaria decided to issue a "Bulgarian medal" to honor the press corps and other important people.

Anton happened to be visiting Saint Petersburg at the time. A Russian diplomat who was monitoring Russian public opinion for Ferdinand asked Anton to recommend people who might be worthy of a medal. Anton and his friend Kolomnin, who was an attorney in Saint Petersburg, were just about to send a silver tea glass–holder to Pokrovsky as a gift, so when Anton heard about the medal, he thought of Pokrovsky right away and gave the diplomat his name.

The elderly archpriest, finding himself overcome with emotion from the receipt of both the glass-holder and the medal, wrote to thank Anton. In the letter, he asked Anton to send him his books to read, writing "Kindly *brownsequard* the old man!" (He was referring to Brown-Séquard, the popular inventor of a supposedly rejuvenating medicine.

So Anton sent him *Motley Stories,* whose title page had the author's name as *A. Chekhonte.* The nickname that Pokrovsky had bestowed on him had become part of

Russian literature! But his prophecy did not come true—a lot of good came out of Anton.

Our Father was also fond of praying, but the more I think about it now, the more I realize that he enjoyed the ritual of religion more than its substance. He liked church services and listened to them standing reverently throughout. He even organized prayers at home, my siblings and I acting as the choir while he played the role of the priest. But the church served more as his club, a place where he could meet his friends, or look at the depiction of a particular saint.

But in everyday life, our Father had as little faith as all the rest of us sinners. He sang, played violin, wore a top hat, and visited friends and family on Easter and Christmas. He loved newspapers, having subscribed for many years, beginning with *The Northern Bee* and *The Son of Motherland*. He collected every issue with care, tying up the entire set at the end of the year and stacking it under the counter of his shop. He always read newspapers out loud from cover to cover. He liked talking about politics and discussing the doings of the town's governor. I never saw him without a starched shirt on. Even when we weren't as well off, he always dressed impeccably. He was intolerant of even a single spot on his clothes and it fell to my sister to ensure he had a pristine shirt each day.

Music was our Father's calling. He would sing or play his violin, meticulously following the adagios and moderatos.

To satisfy this passion, he put together choirs with our family and others and we would perform at home and in public. He would often forget about the business that earned him a living—perhaps that explains why he went broke later. He was also a gifted artist: one of his paintings, "John the Evangelist," made it into the Chekhov Museum in Yalta. For many years, Father served in municipal elections, and he never missed a single ceremony or charity dinner with the local elite. He liked philosophizing, but while Uncle Mitrofan read only books of a lofty content, our Father read and re-read (always out loud) cheap French novels. Sometimes, preoccupied with his own thoughts, he would stop in the middle of a sentence and ask our Mother, "So, Evochka, what was it that I just read?"

I do not know much about Mikhail Emelianovich, our Great-grandfather on my Father's side. According to what Father told us, our Great-grandfather had a brother, Piotr Emelianovich, who raised money to build a church. He traveled on foot through Russia and ended up building a church in Kiev. Our family's recordkeeping starts with our Grandfather Egor Mikhailovich, who lived with his wife, three sons, and daughter, in the village of Olkhovatka, in the Ostrogozh region of the Voronezh province. All of them were serfs of the landowner Chertkov, whose grandson was to become Leo Tolstoy's closest follower.

Our Grandfather had an unquenchable thirst for freedom. He bought himself out of serfdom long before its
abolition, but did not have the means to also free his
daughter Alexandra. He requested the landowner not to
sell her until he could save up the money to buy her freedom too. Chertkov thought a bit, and then said, "Ah, so be
it, take her now." And this is how my dear Aunt Alexandra
Egorovna became free. In Olkhovatka my ancestors bore
the nickname *Chekh,* not Chekhov, and their love of freedom allowed my romantic Uncle to believe in the following
fable, which he often retold.

Uncle would say, "Our ancestor was likely a Czech born
in Bohemia who fled to Russia because of religious perse-
cution. He would have had to seek the protection of someone in power, and was probably forced to become a serf. Or
maybe he married a serf and due to the law at the time—or
of his own volition—he made his children serfs too." Then
my romantic Uncle would add: "I think so, my dear, because if he were a simple peasant, how would he have managed to run away from his native land? No, no, he must
have been an important and noble man."

Uncle Mitrofan believed this fanciful idea about our
ancestor until the day he died. We would just grin when
we heard it because we knew another version of the story
of where we came from and this one was documented.
The famous Tsar-Cannon, now in the Moscow Kremlin,
was cast in 1586 by a master-smelter named Andrey
Chekhov. But did it mean that we were descended from
him?

OUR Grandfather sent his eldest son Mikhail to apprentice to a book-binder in Kaluga, while he moved with his
other two sons, our Father, Pavel, and our Uncle Mitrofan,
to Count Platov's immense estates near Taganrog and Rostov-on-Don, where he had become manager. His daughter
Alexandra was married by now and remained in Olkhovatka. This is how my Father and Uncle wound up in the
far south, on the shores of the Sea of Azov. My Father became a shop assistant to Kobylin, a merchant and the
mayor of Taganrog, while my Uncle went to work for a merchant named Baidalakov in Rostov before eventually returning to Taganrog. Having spent the required years with
Kobylin, my Father, Pavel Egorovich, then opened his own
shop of colonial goods and married our Mother, Evgenia
Yakovlevna Morozova.[8]

We didn't know who our maternal great-grandfather
was. Our Mother's father, Yakov Gerasimovich Morozov,
lived in Morshansk in the Tambov province, where he married Alexandra Ivanovna. They had two daughters,
Fenichka and our Mother, Evochka, and one son Ivan, our
Uncle Vanya. Yakov Gerasimovich had a well-developed
textile trade with the French and often took long business
trips, which sometimes brought him to Taganrog, a capital
of the south at that time. He would stay in General Papkov's house, adjacent to the Alexander I Palace garden.

Once while her husband was away traveling, our maternal Grandmother, Alexandra Ivanovna, decided to
take her two daughters and son to Shuya to visit her sister Maria Ivanovna, who had married a man from an Old

Believers[9] family in Shuya in the Vladimir province. While they were away, our Grandfather Yakov Gerasimovich died in a cholera outbreak in Novocherkassk, far from his home and family. It was presumed that he must have had some textile goods and some money with him when he died, so our Grandmother took the children, rented a horse-drawn carriage, and ventured all the way from Shuya to Novocherkassk, some 800 miles south, to look for her husband's grave.

The trip left an indelible impression on my Mother and Aunt. They would have traveled through dense primeval forests and encountered inns fortified with prison-style gates, heard of or witnessed robberies and murders of traveling merchants and endured countless other trials. Only once they made it to the expanse and freedom of the steppes near the Azov would they have been able to sleep under the open sky, close to nature, and no longer have had to live in fear of evil men or assaults. This trip provided our Mother and Fenichka with an inexhaustible source of family stories to tell us when we were little, stories to which we listened wide-eyed, holding our breath. Both Auntie and Mother were perceptive women and excellent storytellers. I am sure that their stories played an important role in the development of my brothers' imaginations and literary sensibilities.

Alexandra Ivanovna never found her husband's grave in Novocherkassk nor any material possessions to remind her of him. She never returned to Morshansk, moving her children to Taganrog instead and settling down at General

Papkov's, where her husband used to stay. Stopping at Rostov-on-Don on her way, she arranged for her son Ivan to work for Baidalakov's business, which is how our Uncle Ivan met Mitrofan who, as I have mentioned, also worked for Baidalakov. Both were big dreamers and they soon became good friends, remaining close until Uncle Vanya's death from consumption.

Once Mitrofan had grown into a young man, he moved to Taganrog and opened his own business and Uncle Vanya soon followed. It was through him and Mitrofan that our Father met the Morozovs and married the younger daughter Evgenia. Uncle Vanya, the artistic soul, the musician who could play all kinds of instruments, the painter and polyglot, then married Marfa Ivanovna Loboda, our favorite aunt.

My Father married my Mother on October 26, 1854, when the Sebastopol War was just beginning. During their first year of marriage, they lived at my maternal grandparents' house. I assume that the Chekhovs and the Morozovs were living together at the time, because of the family lore of the British bombardment of Taganrog in the summer of 1855 and the effect it had on our extended family. That summer, on the eve of Kazanskaya,[10] our Grandmother Alexandra Ivanovna was attending vespers, conducted by Father Aleksey Sharkov, when all of a sudden a bomb blew in the wall, shaking the entire church and scattering plaster. The scared parishioners crowded together while Father Aleksey, his hands trembling, continued to read. By the time the service ended and the terrified parishioners had filed out of the church, the departing British ships' pale silhouettes were barely visible on the horizon.

They returned on July 26. The night before Father Aleksey Sharkov came to our Grandmother Alexandra Ivanovna and warned her that the white ships had appeared on the horizon again. He had climbed the bell tower and seen the white ships anchored offshore. He recommended that she take my Mother, then pregnant with my older brother Alexander, away from the city. The next day was Sunday and my Father and Uncle went to church. After the liturgy, they climbed the cliffs above the shore where they could see the British squadron. As they stood awestruck in front of the impressive fleet, the ships fired a salvo. Terrified, my Father rolled down the cliff while Uncle Vanya ran home as fast as he could.

Back at the house, Alexandra Ivanovna had just put on chicken soup, the samovar was heating up, and my Mother was in bed. As bombs began to fly over the city, local hooligans started barging into homes breaking mirrors and furniture, ostensibly so nothing would be left for the enemy. My Mother and Grandmother did not know what to do. Uncle Vanya probably did not either as, according to them, he grabbed the boiling samovar and began pouring out the hot water. Just then my Father rushed in with a peasant cart that he had picked up along the way. They put my Grandmother, my pregnant Mother, and Fenichka in it and, leaving everything behind, headed out of the city. As she rode along, listening to the distant shots, Alexandra Ivanovna kept sighing and murmuring, "What about the chicken . . .

my chicken will be overcooked." They stopped at the village of Krepkaya, forty miles from Taganrog, where they stayed with Father Kitaisky, the local priest, and my Mother gave birth to her first son, Alexander, on August 10.

Alexander was interesting and highly educated, a very kind, gentle, and compassionate man. He was a marvelous linguist, an original philosopher, and endowed with literary talents. He wrote under the pen name A. Sedoy. He reported on scientific meetings in newspapers, and thanks to his broad knowledge, lecturers frequently requested that he cover their talks. Many professors, including the famous A. F. Koni, often delayed their presentations to wait for him. However, the disquieting days leading up to his birth—under enemy fire, so to speak—left a legacy. He suffered from sustained and frequent periods of heavy drinking. He wrote prodigiously during these periods, but once sober would look on the work with distaste. His recollections about Anton Chekhov's childhood, for example, contain very little truth. But when he was well, when he was again the real, sweet, exciting Alexander, listening to him was pure joy. He was a walking encyclopedia and a conversation with him about any topic was incredibly interesting. He died in 1913, leaving a son, my godchild Mikhail Chekhov, the well-known actor of the Moscow Art Theater.[11]

In May 1857, my parents had their second son, Nikolay, the future artist. He was also highly gifted: talented on both the violin and piano, a serious painter, and an original caricaturist. He participated in exhibitions with some huge paintings (*Strolling in Sokolniky* and *Messalina*) and his works were displayed in the former Church of Christ the Savior. His drawings and caricatures were elegant and witty. Several of his paintings were collected in the Chekhov Museum in Moscow and one painting and two or three watercolors were exhibited in the Yalta Museum. He died in his prime, at only thirty-one.[12] He now rests in peace at the Luchansky Cemetery near Sumy in the Kharkov province.

On January 17, 1860 Anton Chekhov, the future famous writer, was born. A year later came Ivan, who became a well-known teacher in Moscow. My sister Maria Pavlovna and I followed.[13]

II

OUR
CHILDHOOD
IN TAGANROG

By the time I was old enough to be aware of my surroundings and had learned to read street signs from my brothers, Alexander was already in fifth grade, Nikolay was in third, and Anton and Ivan were in first. We lived at the Moiseev house on the corner of Monastyrsky Street and Yarmorochny Alley then, almost at the very edge of the city. We occupied a big two-story house with a yard that contained a few sheds. Our Father's shop and the kitchen, dining room, and two other rooms were on the first floor. Our family and our tenants lived upstairs. One of the tenants who boarded with us was a man named Gavriil Parfentievich Selivanov, and the other was an eighth-grade student, Ivan Yakovlevich Pavlovsky.

Pavlovsky later enrolled in the Medical Academy in Saint Petersburg, and earned some notoriety when he was

arrested and charged in the infamous Trial of the 193,[1] and
imprisoned in the Peter and Paul Fortress. He managed
to escape while being deported to Siberia and fled to
America. He worked for a time as a barber in New York
and wrote about it to the director of Taganrog school,
who reported this modest achievement to his students
with great disappointment. Pavlovsky then moved to
Paris, where he published an article in a local paper about
his time in the Peter and Paul Fortress. The famous writer
Ivan Turgenev,[2] who lived in Paris then, saw the article and
took Pavlovsky under his wing. With Turgenev's support,
Pavlovsky began writing in French and Russian, and soon
became a well-known writer. He wrote under the pen
name of I. Yakovlev and actively contributed to the newspaper *New Time,* where he had a satirical column on life
in Paris. He also reported on the famous Dreyfus affair.
His books included *Little People with Big Grief* and the
very interesting *Spanish Essays* (both published in 1889).
Many years later, when Anton was already a famous writer
and living in Melikhovo, he heard that Pavlovsky had received amnesty. He came to see my brother at his estate
and the two of them reminisced about the old days in
Taganrog.

The Malaksiano family lived next door. They were a
Russian Greek family with two daughters and a son named
Afonia. I befriended Afonia while the two girls played with
my sister, Masha. One of the girls grew up to become a
prominent revolutionary; she was convicted and sentenced
to hard labor. According to Anton, after she slapped the

camp warden across the face in response to an insult, she received corporal punishment and died soon after.[3]

From the windows of our corner house we could see Yarmarochny Alley, which connected Yarmarochny and Mitrofanievsky Squares. The new marketplace was on Mitrofanievsky Square, where they also held public executions. On execution days, a black platform with a post would appear, and a lot of people would gather in the square to watch. Accompanied by a drumbeat, the tall black chariot carrying the unfortunate criminal would pass by our windows. The criminal's arms would be tied behind his back, and a blackboard identifying his crime would be hanging from his neck. The procession would stop beside the platform and the criminal would be tied to the post. Then they would read his sentence aloud and, if he was a nobleman, his sword would be broken in half above his head. We would all watch this from the upper floor windows, with our Mother, Evgenia Yakovlevna, sighing deeply and crossing herself. She believed that even criminals were worthy of compassion and that they were oppressed by the powerful, and she instilled in us this attitude.

In general, a feeling of compassion toward criminals was strong in our family. On his saint's day, Uncle Mitrofan always sent baskets of French bread to the prison—a loaf for each convict. Every year on October 24, the feast day, our Mother would go to the all-night vigil at the jail's chapel to talk to the convicts about what they needed and listen to their stories of why they were in jail.

I remember one evening in particular when our Mother went to the jail's chapel and was gone a very long time. Everyone started to worry, so our nanny, Agafia Alexanderovna, took me with her to the gate to wait for Mother to come home. It was twilight and, on the other side of the street, a young girl was hurrying to get home. Suddenly a carriage flew by us and stopped beside the girl. Two men jumped out, grabbed her, and sped away, right in front of our eyes. The terrified girl screamed at the top of her lungs, "Save me! Help me!" I heard her voice for a long time until it finally faded away in the nearby steppe. Not a single person came out or showed any interest at all! Agafia Alexanderovna only scratched her head with her knitting needle, sighed, and murmured: "A girl got abducted." I was too young to understand what had happened, but I later learned that the abduction of young girls for Turkish harems was very common in our city.

We moved into our own house in 1874. Our Father built it on a godforsaken street named Elisavetinsky, on a piece of land given to him by Grandfather Egor Mikhailovich. The house turned out to be awkward and cramped, with extra-thick walls—the contractors used more material than necessary because they got paid by the brick. As a result, the contractors made a large profit, while our Father was left with debt and a low-quality house.

The entire family was squeezed into four small rooms. Our widowed Aunt, Fedosia Yakovlevna, lived in the basement with her son Aliosha. In order to increase our income, one little wing was rented out to the widow Savich.

The widow had a daughter, Iraida, and a son, Anatoly. Anton was friends with Anatoly, and Iraida seems to have been the future writer's first love.

It was a strange yet typical kind of love. They always argued and made caustic remarks to each other. Watching them together, one might have supposed that the fourteen-year-old Anton was poorly mannered. One Sunday, Iraida came out of the house dressed for church and looking graceful as a butterfly. When she passed Anton, he grabbed an empty charcoal bag from the ground and hit her with it. The dust settled over her lovely straw hat like a dark cloud.

Another time, she wrote a touching poem on the garden fence. Anton immediately replied, in chalk, with the following stanza:

> *Oh the poetess of the fence,*
> *Baby toys are still your friends.*
> *Quit your scribbling on the walls,*
> *Just stay home and play with dolls.*

Like many other provincial families of the time, ours was patriarchal. It was also a family that valued education and appreciated spiritual wealth and culture. At his wife's insistence, Pavel Egorovich sought to give his children the broadest education possible. However, as a man of his times, he couldn't decide in which direction he should steer his children.

Given that rich Greeks were the cream of Taganrog's society, spending money like water and putting on airs, our

Father was convinced that his children should follow the Greek model, even possibly completing their education at Athens University. There was a prestigious Greek school in Taganrog where he sent his three older sons—Alexander, Nikolay, and Anton. Despite our Father's blind faith in everything Greek, the instruction there apparently struck him as utterly preposterous, so he decided to send his children to regular school instead. In truth, there is nothing firmly verifiable in our family recollections about my brothers' time at that Greek school. And as far as what my late brother Alexander published in *The European Herald*, I will only repeat that one has to be very careful about his writings.

Our days, which began early, would start and end in work. The boys went to school, came back, and did their homework. When they had a free hour, Alexander made electrical batteries, Nikolay drew, Ivan bound books, and Anton made up stories. Then Father would return home from his shop, and choir practice would begin. Father sang, sight-reading from a music sheet, and taught us how to sing as well. He would sometimes play violin duets with Nikolay, Masha accompanying them on piano, while Mother, always busy, fussed around doing chores or sewed something for us on her machine. She was always full of love and affection. Even though she was still a relatively young woman, she deprived herself of many things in order to dedicate her life fully to her children.

Our Mother was very fond of the theater but unable to go very often. When she did attend, my elder brothers would go along to make sure she got home safely. Mother would sit in the orchestra while my brothers went up to the gallery. At the end of each act, Anton would shout out the names of—not the actors, as was the custom—the Greek aristocrats sitting alongside his Mother in the orchestra. The entire audience would join in and the Greeks would feel so uncomfortable that they would sometimes leave before the end of the show.

Mother was adamantly against serfdom in Russia and would tell us how landowners abused their peasants. She instilled in us a deep sense of love and respect, not only for those who were socially below us but also for birds and animals and all helpless creatures. Anton once said that "we got talent from our Father and soul from our Mother," although I personally believe that much talent came to us from Mother's side, as well.

Madame Chopin, a Frenchwoman, came to teach us languages. Father and Mother attached a lot of importance to languages, and one of my first memories is of my two eldest brothers jabbering at one another in fluent French. When we were older, we had a music teacher who was an official from the local branch of a government bank. We were a typical family caught up in trying to better itself.

As I have said, our Father was strict about everything related to the church. We were not allowed to miss a single Saturday-night vigil or Sunday liturgy, which explains why Anton exhibited such a thorough knowledge of church services in his story "Easter Eve"[4] and others. For a while we sang at the church in the local royal palace, where Tsar

Alexander I lived and died. The services there were held only during Holy Week, on the first day of Easter and on Trinity.*

Our Father spent so much of his time singing, going to church, and working on the elections that he often had to send one of us to the shop "to keep an eye on things" in his stead. Needless to say, he was not a good businessman; he conducted his deals without any real interest and only did business because that was what he was supposed to do. It would have been improper to not open the shop, so the children were sent there because it needed, as they said, "a thrifty master's eye." Father paid his fees for the Third Merchant Guild because our Mother insisted, since membership could help the boys avoid military draft. But as soon as conscription was ordered in 1874 and the guild dissolved, Father became simply a petit bourgeois. If he had been fortunate enough to be placed on the right track in his childhood, he might have been the director of a church choir or a professional opera singer.

Even though we had to work in the shop, we enjoyed many activities that other boys in bigger cities could not imagine. We spent entire days fishing, we played *lapta*,[5] and we put on plays at home. Despite the relative strictness of the family regimen and the occasional corporal punishment (common in those days), we had quite a lot of free-

---

* A. Sedoy's assertion that Anton sang in the palace along with smiths is incorrect, as the smiths, who were members of the church choir, sang at the Mitrofanievsky Church, not the palace.

dom. We could walk out of the house without asking anyone's permission; we just needed to be on time for dinner
or other family occasions. We were always diligent about
our family responsibilities.

I remember our parents arranging one long trip for us: to
the village of Krinichka, forty-three miles from Taganrog.
We had been preparing for this trip for a long time. Age
eighteen, Alexander had made himself a wide-brimmed
paper hat from a sugar bag. Fifteen-year-old Nikolay had
found himself a spring-loaded opera hat to travel in—
which prompted Anton's good-natured but endless mocking. Our Mother had baked and cooked plenty of food for
the road, of course.

We hired a driver named Ivan Fiodorovich. We covered
his cart with pillows, blankets, and a rug and somehow
managed to squeeze all seven of us, plus the driver, into the
cart and get under way. I can scarcely imagine how we had
enough room on that one cart to travel the forty-three
miles there and another forty-three miles back. Nikolay
did not take off his opera hat once, patiently enduring
Anton's mocking. From early childhood, one of Nikolay's
eyes was crossed, and he would keep his head tilted slightly
to one side. This gave Anton particular license, and he
would call Nikolay names and tease him, saying things like,
"Hey Cross-Eye, gimme a smoke! Mr. Wry-Eye, have you
got any tobacco?"

We arrived at Krinichka at sunset. It was a nondescript village, except that near the church there was a well whose very cold water was widely thought to have healing properties. Next to the well stood a tent where people could pour buckets of water from the miraculous well over themselves. As we rolled into Krinichka, Anton, who had been pestering Nikolay with his jokes the whole way, finally managed to knock his opera hat off. It fell under one of the wheels and was immediately crushed, its springs poking out through the fabric.

Nikolay wasn't bothered; he picked it up and put it on again while Alexander called out, "Hey! Go tell the priest that the archbishop's choir has arrived!" No sooner had we found a peasant's house where we could stay than Alexander and Anton had located a fishing net and gone off to the river. They caught five pikes and about fifty crayfish, and Mother concocted a wonderful bisque for us the next day.

We stayed in Krinichka for two days and then continued on to our Grandfather's place in Knyazhaya, about twelve miles away. Our Grandfather Egor Mikhailovich was still working as the manager for Count Platov, who was the son of a well-known soldier and hero of the 1812 war. Knyazhaya was a desolate estate near the river, with an expansive fruit orchard. Grandfather and Grandmother lived in a small hut. They had built it for themselves near the absent owner's big manor because Grandfather did not wish to live "in the mansion." When we arrived, Anton and Nikolay, who had visited the place the year before during the harvest, felt right at home. My brothers and I were given places to sleep in the big house. But we hardly got a minute's rest because, despite being vacant of human residents for decades, it turned out to be full of fleas.

Yet our stay in Knyazhaya was a happy one, and we enjoyed the smithy, the threshing barn, the pigeons, the orchard, the open space, and most important, the complete absence of any responsibilities. As for the wretched opera hat, it soon met its end. Nikolay could not be parted from his treasure, even to go swimming. So, naked but still wearing the hat, Nikolay was wading in the river when Anton sneaked up behind him and knocked the hat off. It fell into the river, took in some water, and disappeared.

WHEN it came to new ideas, Anton was really the most talented at dreaming them up, but he was also the least inclined to do any physical work. He would organize lectures and plays, and was always performing something or imitating someone. But I never once saw him bind a book, take apart a clock, or do any physical work the way my other brothers did.

There was one rare occasion when even Anton showed some interest in manual labor. In 1874, the Taganrog district college offered occupational classes taught by a man named Porumb. He was a jack of all trades: he could repair sewing machines, build boots, and tailor clothes. He had a beard so long that he used it to sweep leather trimmings off the work board he kept on his lap. The occupational classes were free, so my brothers all decided to learn a craft. Ivan took classes in bookbinding and Anton began studying tailoring. Soon, the writer-to-be was presented with an opportunity to test his skills in real life: making a new pair of gray pants for Nikolay to wear to school. With the air of a true expert, Anton bravely picked up the scissors. Narrow pants were in style at the time, so Nikolay kept hovering over him giving advice: "A bit more narrow, Anton—no one wears wide any more—come now—make it narrower." So Anton cut out a pair of pants so narrow that Nikolay could barely get them on. After a struggle, he eventually managed to pull them up. To complete the outfit, he put on some fancy shoes and walked out of the house.

"Hey, look at him!" boys on the street said, pointing. "Wow! Boots like ships, pants like noodles!"

From then on, the expression "noodle-pants" had a permanent place in our family's vocabulary.

Anton was the expert when it came to doing home theater. When we were young, we put on Gogol's *The Inspector General* as well as shows in Ukrainian about Chuprun and his wife Chuprunikha, with Anton playing the lead.[6] One of his favorite scenes was the one in which the town's mayor goes to the cathedral on a holiday and stands on the little rug in the middle of the church among foreign consuls.

During this time, our eldest brother Alexander was living at the school director's house and did not participate in family events. He was already considered a grown-up. In 1875 he finished school, left for Moscow, and never came back. Nikolay left with him, bringing our home theater to an end, and leaving Anton to inherit the mantle of authority. The Chekhov family was reduced to the three younger brothers and one sister. The four of us were destined to remain together for a long time, until the mid-1890s.

THAT same year, Anton fell seriously ill and almost died. As I mentioned before, Gavriil Parfentievich had been our boarder for a few years. During the day he worked as a clerk at the commercial court, but he passed his nights over high-stakes gambling at a club. He had so much luck that, ten years later, he was able to buy himself horses and a large estate. His brother, Ivan Parfentievich, was also a gambler, but a less lucky one. Since he did not have a single kopeck to his name, he was hoping to marry rich. Finally, the fates aligned and he found an older woman, a widow, who had a large estate of about 800 acres in the Donetsk coalfield. Ivan Parfentievich invited Anton to visit them there. Either on his way to the estate or on his way back, Anton swam in a cold river and caught a serious cold. "Antosha fell sick on me," Ivan Parfentievich told me twenty years later, "and I had no idea what to do with him. So I took him to the Jewish inn and we put him to bed there."

I remember vividly how close to death's door Anton looked when he was brought home. I can still picture the scene—Dr. Shtrempf muttering, with a German accent, "Antosha, if you vish being healthy . . ."; Mother, anxiously frying linseed for a poultice; and me running to the pharmacy for pills, every one of which bore the name of its inventor, Covin. Later, when he was a physician himself, Anton often said that those pills were absolutely useless.

It was Anton's first brush with a serious illness and it left a profound mark. The inn where Ivan Parfentievich took him was used in his story "Steppe." The characters Moisey Moiseevich and his wife and brother Solomon were based on the inn's owners. And the illness brought him so close to Dr. Shtrempf that Anton decided to follow in his footsteps and study medicine at Dorpat University, where Shtrempf had received his degree. If our family had not moved to Moscow, he really might have followed his dream to go to Dorpat.

AFTER Alexander and Nikolay left home for Moscow, Father could barely make ends meet. His business was failing once and for all. We felt isolated and aware of our reduced circumstances. Although we lived in our own house, we were plagued by debt. During the day, all of us boys worked very hard. In the evenings, Antosha would entertain us with his improvised sketches or we would listen to stories told by Mother, Aunt Fedosia Yakovlevna, or our nanny, Agafia Alexanderovna Kumskaya. The nanny lived with us for a long time and left only when we were about to leave Taganrog. She was a wonderful woman who told stories of her rich life remarkably well. She started her life as a serf of the Ilovaiskys, a well-known family in the south, where she worked as a companion to General Ilovaisky's only daughter. She once went on a long trip with her and helped the daughter run away from home to marry Baron Rozen against her father's wishes, after which Agafia was sold to another family. Her stories were mostly about mysterious and unusual things and were very poetic. Anton's story "Happiness" was undoubtedly influenced by her stories.[7]

In 1876, Father finally closed his business and ran away to Moscow to avoid debtor's prison. He joined his two elder sons there; Alexander was enrolled at university and Nikolay studied in the College of Painting, Sculpture, and Architecture. With Father gone, Anton became the head of the family.

I remember that time in my life very well. That summer was especially hot and sleeping indoors was impossible, so we set up tents in the yard and slept there. Since Anton slept under a vine he had planted, he called himself "Job under the fig tree." We would wake up early and Anton would take me with him to the market to buy the day's food.

Once, he bought a live duck at the market. He kept poking at it and making it quack the whole way home — "Let everybody hear that we, too, eat ducks," he said. Anton liked looking at the pigeons at the market, expertly evaluating their feathers and deciding their worth. He owned some pigeons, which he let out of the pigeon house every morning. He seemed to truly enjoy them.

Finances became so tight that Ivan and I were sent to live with our Grandfather in Knyazhaya to reduce the number of mouths the family had to feed. Right after that, we experienced a family catastrophe—we lost our house.

The house had been built on a very tight budget, with the last 500 rubles borrowed from the mutual loan society. The promissory note was guaranteed by Kostenko, an employee of the society. The note was passed around for a long time until Father finally had to declare himself insolvent.

Kostenko paid for the note and brought a counterclaim against Father in commercial court. In those days, insolvents were sent to debtor's prison so, as I said before, Father had to run away. He boarded a train—not in Taganrog, but at a nearby stop where he wouldn't be recognized.

Our friend Gavriil Parfentievich worked in the commercial court where Kostenko had brought his case against my Father. We thought it was a stroke of luck when Gavriil Parfentievich decided to pay father's debt and save the house from auction for us. "I will do this for my Mother and sister," he announced to our Mother (he always referred to our Mother and sister as if they were his own). But what he really did was secure the house for himself, as the owner. He did it right there, at the court, without announcing a public auction, and he did it for only 500 rubles.

While Gavriil Parfentievich made plans to take possession of our house, Kostenko was allowed to remove all our furnishings as payment on the interest due. Our Mother was left with nothing. What could she do but leave Taganrog? In tears, she boarded the train and took Masha and me to Moscow. We were going to rejoin our Father and brothers, but it was hardly a joyous occasion. We were heading into the unknown.

Anton and Ivan were left behind in Taganrog. Anton stayed at the house to keep it safe until the new owner moved in, and Ivan was temporarily taken in by our Aunt Marfa Ivanovna. Ivan was soon sent to Moscow as well, leaving Anton all alone in Taganrog.

When Gavriil Parfentievich moved into the house, he offered to let Anton stay if he would tutor his nephew Petia Kravtsov before he left for military school. Petia was the son of a Cossack landowner from the Donetsk district who had spent some time serving in the Caucasus. Since they were almost the same age, Anton and Petia became friends. When summer came, Petia invited him to their estate. I remember how excitedly Anton recounted his time in the steppe to me, and how much he liked living with such an unpretentious family.

Anton learned how to shoot a gun there and to enjoy hunting. He also became skilled at riding stallions. He told me that their dogs were so mean that he would have to wake up the owners in order to use the outhouse at night. Apparently, the dogs were never fed and had to forage for their own food. No one counted the poultry, either; wild chicks roamed in and out, and because they had never been handled by humans, they could not be caught with bare hands. For dinner, the wild chickens had to be shot with a gun.

Meanwhile, it was the dawn of the coal and railway era. Many details of that period wound up in Anton's writing—from the sound of a falling bucket in the mine in *The Cherry Orchard* to the railroad embankment being built in "The Lights" to the loose cargo car rolling by itself in "Fears."[8]

Before we all moved to Moscow, Gavriil Parfentievich's niece Sasha, who was a student in the women's school, had slept in my sister's room as a boarder. The boys were all friends with her, but Anton used to make her cry by calling her "The Bug," thanks to a red dress with black spots that she wore. After we left for Moscow, she moved in with her Uncle, who eventually moved back into our house. She visited us in Moscow twenty years later, when we lived in the Korneev house on Kudrinskaya-Sadovaya Street. Sasha had grown up to be merry and cheerful, and she loved singing Ukrainian songs. Both Anton and Ivan flirted with her for the entire month she stayed with us. I wrote poems in her diary and composed versed epigrams about my brothers. They would tease her about her potential suitors, saying that one was anxiously awaiting her in the south. I remember a practical joke Anton played on her. He took an old telegram, erased the lines written in pencil and wrote in their place, "Angel, sweetheart, missing you terribly, come back soon, waiting for my beloved. Your lover." Then they called from the lobby pretending to be the mailman, and the housemaid handed Sasha the telegram.

She opened it, read it, and although we begged her to stay, she went home the next day. We tried to explain to her that the telegram was a fake, but she did not believe us. She came to visit us much later in Melikhovo, after she had become a widow. She was still infectiously cheerful and still sang Ukrainian songs. Imitating her, Anton Pavlovich used to say, "Hey, sister, why worry about a thing!"

DURING his lonely stay in Taganrog from 1876 to 1879, Anton visited his friend V. I. Zembulatov at his estate. Anton liked giving his school friends nicknames, and he called this plump boy "Makar."[9] Even though Zembulatov went on to become an esteemed doctor, the nickname always stuck. Anton remembered their summer vacations fondly.

I was separated from Anton for three years after I moved to Moscow in 1876, so unfortunately I can't illuminate much about those years in this biography. It is a pity because it is during that time that he really matured, formed his character, and turned from boy to young man.

As far as I know, he began dating girls when he was in seventh and eighth grade. When I was in eighth grade, he told me that his love affairs were always a lot of fun. When he was a university student and I was still a schoolboy, he would give me a nudge, point at some girl passing by, and say, "Go, go after her! She's a great find for a seventh-grader!"

Anton attended theater performances often during those years in Taganrog. He liked French melodramas like *The Koverly Murder* and merry French farces like *Mama's Boy.* He also read a lot. The book *Hammer and Anvil* by Friedrich Spielhagen and the novels of Victor Hugo and Georg Born made an especially strong impression on him. In this time, he wrote a drama called *Without a Father*[10] and a vaudeville called *The Chicken Didn't Sing in Vain.*[11] While in school, he subscribed to the newspaper *The Son of Motherland* and wrote a handwritten magazine with caricatures called *Stutterer.* He portrayed his brothers in Moscow satirically in the magazine and sent it along to let us in on his joke.

Years later, after Anton's death, Aleksey S. Suvorin[12] shared the following episode of Anton's life with me. Apparently, Anton was staring at his reflection in the water of a remote well at someone's steppe estate when a girl of about fifteen came to get water. She fascinated him so much that he could not help but kiss her. They both stood beside the well for a long time, looking at the water in complete silence. He did not want to leave and she had forgotten her original reason for being there. Anton told Suvorin about this episode during a conversation they had about personal compatibility and love at first sight.

I I I

THE EARLY
YEARS IN
MOSCOW

OUR MOTHER, MY SISTER, AND I ARRIVED IN MOSCOW ON
July 26, 1876. Since Taganrog was a new city with neat
buildings and straight avenues lined with trees, I expected
Moscow to be the same, only grander. Our home always
had pictures of London, Paris, and Venice hanging on the
walls. The picture of Venice showed the Grand Canal filled
with gondolas and its banks lined with palaces. It had an
inscription in three languages: *Vue de Venice Aussicht von
Venedig,* and in Russian, "A Morning in Venice." My childhood self came to understand that a country's chief cities
would be beautiful and elegant—an incarnation of high
culture.

I felt such surprise and disappointment when our train
arrived at the shabby Kursky Terminal in Moscow! It

looked like a barn compared with the Taganrog station. Outside I glimpsed filthy sidewalks, low and dilapidated buildings, oddly crooked streets, numerous unsightly churches, and cab drivers dressed so raggedly that they would have been scorned in Taganrog. I already knew the Kremlin and the Sukharev Tower from pictures (for many years a collection of pictures of Moscow, called "The Bee" published by Shcherbina, occupied a place of honor on our table, alongside another favorite, *The Children of Captain Grant*). But even the Kremlin and the Sukharev Tower disappointed me.

Our Father and Nikolay met us at the station, but we had to walk all the way to our apartment in Grachiovka because Father did not have six kopecks to spare for a horse-drawn tram. He did not have a job yet, and my brothers were both penniless, too. From the very beginning, our financial situation defined our life in Moscow.

Our first order of business was to sell the silver spoons and silver ruble coins that Mother had brought with her. We lived in one room and Alexander, Nikolay, and I slept in the closet under the stairway. We had to switch from southern wheat bread to rye, which was a particular blow for me because I disliked rye bread so much. Having left all of our old household items behind, we had to run to a nearby shop for every little thing, and I was quickly made an errand boy. Meanwhile, my poor eleven-year-old sister was put in charge of the family's washing and ironing, which included starching all of our Father's and elder brothers' shirts.

Those first three impoverished years in Moscow were pure suffering for all of us.

Used to the spaciousness of Taganrog, I felt cramped and terribly homesick. I would regularly walk from our apartment all the way back to the Kursky station to watch the arrival of the southern trains. I would speak to those dear cars that I knew came from Taganrog, asking them to take my warm regards back to my city.

Meanwhile, Anton's frequent letters from Taganrog were filled with good humor and support. They vanished somewhere between our various Moscow apartments, which is a shame because they would have shed more light on his personal development. In his letters Anton would encourage me to read and recommend certain books, and he would send various riddles like, "Why does a goose swim?" or "What kind of stones are found in the sea?" He promised to bring me a trained hawfinch when he came to Moscow. He once sent us a parcel with tall boots filled with tobacco for my brothers. He tried to sell the last of our belongings in Taganrog (some jars and pots) and sent us what little money he could get for them. He and Mother would correspond about these sales; she never used punctuation and would start her letters with lines like: "Antosha on the shelf in the pantry," and Anton would poke gentle fun at her, replying "After a long search, no Antosha was found on the pantry shelf."

During those early days in Moscow, education was a serious problem for my sister and me. I had completed first grade and my sister second, but when classes started on August 16, we had to stay home because there was no money for school. We would have needed twenty-five rubles each, and at that point in our lives, there was no way to get it.

August and September passed, then the cold weather moved in unusually early that year, but my sister and I still stayed home. I began to feel truly alarmed when I overheard conversations about placing me as an errand boy in Gavrilov's warehouse (the one described in Anton's novel *Three Years*.[1] My cousin was already working there and he could have easily recommended me. I was terrified and so, without saying a word to anyone, I snuck out of the house and ran to the Third School on Lubianka. They refused to accept me. I did not know the city or its schools that well, but I ran for miles toward the familiar Kursky station and from there found my way to the Second School on Razguliay.

Working up my courage, I walked in, climbed the stairs, and crossed the assembly hall to a desk covered in green cloth—the director was sitting there, alone. I could hear the familiar din of students from the nearby classes in the background. I walked up to the director and—in my southern accent—told him why I was there. I tried to be very polite and asked him to please accept me into his school. I told him how much I wanted to study and about the threat of Gavrilov's warehouse.

His turned to me and asked, "Why didn't your parents come?" I made up a plausible excuse. He thought for a while and then said, "All right, I will take you in. You can

start school tomorrow—only tell someone from your family to come and sign you up."

I ran the whole way home! My family was ecstatic
when I told them that I was going to be a student again. I
had secured my reputation; my parents loved to repeat,
"Misha has enrolled in school—all by himself!"

The winter was harsh and my overcoat thin. I often
cried on my two-mile walk to and from school because of
the unbearable cold. The question of paying for my school
was soon resolved, though. One of my Father's odd jobs at
the time was as a scribe at the Gavrilov warehouse. The
warehouse was in a central area of the city called Warm
Booths and I usually ran to the warehouse to help him after
school. An out-of-town trader there who bought goods
from Gavrilov often talked to me and asked questions.
When he died that winter, it turned out that he had left
me a stipend of fifty rubles a year for my education.

Gavrilov was the executor of the trader's estate, and
when it came time to dispense me the money, he would
interrogate me on whether I went to church, whether I
was loyal to the tsar, whether I secretly planned to become a *specivalist* (he meant socialist), and so on. I found
his charity offensive, so as soon as I started making my
own money in fifth grade, I stopped accepting what I
considered his alms.

We had a wonderful surprise that first Christmas:
Anton came to visit. I showed him the Kremlin and the
capital's other sights, and he got so tired from all the walking that he complained about his sore heels for several days.
Contrary to my expectations, Moscow impressed him very

deeply. He did not have the money to pay for his trip back, so he stayed with us until the beginning of Lent and the Shrovetide celebrations. When he finally went back, he took a doctor's excuse to school, issued by Dr. Yablonovsky with the help of our brother Alexander. While he lived with us, Anton told us all about the Taganrog school, the pranks they dreamed up, and the close relationships they enjoyed with their instructors. All of this made me very jealous, because I was having a rough time in my Moscow school.

Around this time, several attempts had been made to assassinate Alexander II. The revolutionary underground had expanded its activities and society at large had begun openly talking about the benefits of a constitution. This mobilized the reactionaries, and even the youngest students became targets of intense scrutiny as they did their best to knock "socialism" out of us. The Department of Education espoused the absurd doctrine that fear leads to respect and respect always leads to love. Therefore, school administrators set out to instill a senseless fear in students, in this way hoping to inspire our loyalty to the government. Among the teachers surfaced a few zealots of the ideology. Some were seeking promotions, some acted out of stupidity, still others were plainly sadistic—but they all made our lives miserable.

One instructor, whom I'll call K. K. P., would jeer at us and revel in our suffering. He wrote absolutely worthless books and made us buy them for one or two rubles each, so that he could make money. We never even opened them and left their pages uncut. In his classes, he would make his students cry, but the minute a district inspector showed up to observe the class, he word turn meek and groveling. With great pomp, K. K. P. converted from Catholicism (or maybe Uniatism[2]) to Orthodox Christianity. He once picked on a fifth-grade student so ruthlessly that another student, Rakov, who couldn't stand it any more, stood up and yelled, "Oh, K. K. P.! You are an abject rascal!" Of course, Rakov was expelled immediately, but K. K. P. continued to teach classical languages—to the delight of the Department of Education. K. K. P. ruined many of his students' lives and futures.

Another teacher would search students' pockets under the pretext of preventing underage smoking, but would then keep their silver cigarette cases for himself. Y. Kremer (a famous translator of textbooks on classical languages by Kurzius and Kuner, which my brothers and I used in school) once told me the story of how one of his colleagues in the classical languages department showed up on his doorstep at two o'clock in the morning the night before his son's finals. Kremer came downstairs in a robe with a candle. "I played cards tonight and lost," said his visitor, "so give me twenty-five rubles quick!" "But I don't have it," said Kremer. His colleague replied, "Have you forgotten that I am examining your son tomorrow?" Flustered, Kremer went upstairs, retrieved twenty-five rubles from the jewelry box and resignedly gave the money to his destitute colleague.

And yet it was amazing to me the way these same teachers would bristle with self-righteousness over their students' comparatively minor faults, like the time all hell broke loose when two of my classmates, Y. and N., were found in possession of the Nikolay Chernyshevsky novel *What Is to Be Done?*[3]

When Ivan Delianov became the secretary of education, he issued a memo informing administrators that poor children would no longer be allowed to attend school.[4] I was poor, and since my clothes were all patched and stitched, there was a good chance of my being expelled. Teachers were instructed to investigate the private lives of their students, and they could show up at our apartments whenever they wanted, regardless of whether it was bedtime or dinnertime. Given how depressed and circumspect we Moscow students became, Anton's cheerfulness and stories of his friendships with his teachers in Taganrog (part of the Odessa school district, where the terror tactics had not yet reached) sounded like a fairy tale to me.

During this period in Moscow, Anton met and became close to our cousin Mikhail Mikhailovich Chekhov. He was the son of our elder Uncle, Mikhail Egorovich, the one whom our Grandfather Egor Mikhailovich sent to Kaluga to learn the craft of bookbinding. Mikhail Mikhailovich was handsome, honest and kind, and very devoted to his family. He had heard stories about Anton from us and, although he had never met Anton and was much older (he was about thirty then), he wrote him a letter of support and friendship. They corresponded but did not actually meet until Anton's visit to Moscow. Mikhail Mikhailovich also worked in the Gavrilov warehouse, and was Gavrilov's most trusted man, overseeing the company alongside one other clerk (who later formed the basis for the character who called his master a "slave driver" in Anton's novel *Three Years*).

Continuing my sister's education turned out to be more challenging than mine had been. She had missed the application deadlines and because there were no vacancies, couldn't find a place anywhere. Our parents did not handle the situation properly, perhaps because they were over-whelmed by the logistics of managing our large family and by the hardships of work, or maybe because, being provin-cial, they didn't understand how things functioned in Moscow. Luckily, everything turned out all right: my sister managed to get herself enrolled in a school and eventually graduated with a teacher's diploma from the Guerrier School for Higher Education. There she was lucky to at-tend lectures by such luminaries as Professors Klyuchevsky, Karelin, Guerrier, and Storozhenko, and I have wonderful memories of helping her with her lessons. I was then in my senior year of school, feeling suffocated by the discipline and our dry textbooks. Helping her, I found myself enjoy-ing the immersion in an unfamiliar and a new kind of learn-ing, and I believe that my exposure to my sister's lectures had a great deal to do with my future educational path.

Moreover, my sister's schooling changed our family life. Her school friends would gather in our home and read writ-ers like Karl Marx and V. V. Bervi-Flerovsky, who could only be discussed in whispers behind closed doors. Without ex-ception, those sweet girls all grew up to be interesting and intellectual women, and many remained our friends for years. Anton courted one of them, Yunosheva. He would escort her home, and later helped her launch her literary beginnings. He even wrote her a poem:

> *As whimsical as a cigar's smoke*
> > *You have been soaring in my dream,*
> *And dealing many a fateful stroke,*
> > *With fiery smiles your eyes would beam.*

With another girl, who went on to become an astronomer, Anton stayed friends until his death. He introduced her to A. S. Suvorin, and they both helped her a great deal. Anton modeled the character of Rassudina in *Three Years* after her.[5]

After three years of job hunting, our Father was finally offered a full-time position with Gavrilov. It was a desk job, paid thirty rubles a month, and included room and board with the other clerks at Gavrilov's house in Zamoskvorechie District. Seizing the opportunity, our Father moved to the other side of the city.

Our elder brother Alexander had already moved out. Nikolay was attending art school, where he befriended a fellow student, F. Shekhtel[6] (who later became a famous architect, member of the Academy, and designer of the Moscow Art Theater building, among others). Ivan was studying to become a country teacher. There was an addition to our family, too: at our invitation, our Aunt Fedosia Yakovlevna had come from Taganrog to live with us. We were living in dire poverty, barely making ends meet, and with little hope for improvement. During those first three years in Moscow, we lived in twelve different apartments. Eventually, in 1879, we rented a damp space in the basement of Saint Nikolas Church in Grachiovka, with windows that looked out on the feet of passers by.

Anton joined us here after he finished school in Taganrog and came to Moscow to apply to university. It had been three years since we'd seen him, and we were expecting him right after the spring finals. But he did not end up coming until the beginning of August, because something important had kept him in Taganrog. A scholarship of twenty-five rubles per month had just been set up by the city fathers for a Taganrog native to pursue higher education, and he had stayed to secure it. Also, aware of our difficult circumstances, Anton arrived with two boarders in tow, his school friends V. I. Zembulatov and D. T. Saveliev.

I happened to be sunning myself outside the gate when Anton first appeared and did not recognize him at first. I saw a tall young man, speaking in a very deep voice and wearing civilian clothes, get out of a cab. When he saw me, he said, "Good day, Mikhail Pavlovich," and only then did I realize that it was my brother Anton! I shrieked with excitement and ran downstairs to tell Mother. Anton cheerfully followed me into the basement and we all showered him with hugs and kisses. I was immediately dispatched to the telegraph office in Karetny Ryad to send our Father a telegram about Anton's arrival. Zembulatov and Saveliev arrived shortly thereafter, and we had to transform our space to accommodate them. All the newness and change was quite overwhelming. Once they were settled in, I took them to the Kremlin and showed them around Moscow until we all got tired. Our Father came home that night, and we had more fun at dinner than we had had in a long time.

The next day brought another surprise. A man from Viatka showed up at our door with his son. This frail boy, as delicate as a girl, had also come to Moscow to apply to the university. Having heard that we were respectable people, the man wanted to know whether our Mother would take in his son as a boarder. He was a very rich man but so protective of his son's morals that having his son live with a respectable family was more important to him than our dark and shabby flat. The young man's name was Nikolay Ivanovich Korobov, and he quickly became friends with Anton and remained so until the end. Our cramped apartment thus gained four young men at once—all medical students united in their pursuit of science, and all highly decent people. Even though Mother charged them very little and fed them very well, it still meant a vast improvement to our diet and more food for all of us.

The deadline for university applications was August 20. They had to be submitted to the chancellor in a rather repugnant downstairs room in the old administration building on Mokhovaya Street. Anton took me as his guide since he did not yet know Moscow well. We found a filthy, cramped room with a low ceiling, filled with tobacco smoke and crowded with applicants. Expecting something

a little grander, Anton was disappointed by this first encounter with the university. But since he ended up spending most of his time in the medical dissection room and in
the clinic on Rozhdestvenka and infrequently went to the
main campus on Mokhovaya, that initial impression soon
faded. In any case, he worked so hard and shouldered so
much responsibility for our family he had little time to
dwell on feelings.

That autumn, we all moved to a new apartment, still in
Grachiovka, but this time on the second floor of the Savitsky house. It was there that Anton began his literary career. Zembulatov and Korobov lived in one room; Saveliev
in another; Nikolay, Anton, and I in the third; our Mother
and sister in the fourth; and the fifth room served as a sitting room for everybody. Since Father lived at Gavrilov's,
Anton once again became the head of the family, making all
the decisions. He spoke in a new way, using phrases that
were decisive and even curt: "It's not true"; "One must be
fair"; "We can't lie." Working together, we slowly began to
improve the family's financial situation. Everybody worked
hard. Every morning, I woke at five to go buy the day's food
for the family. Then I would quickly drink my tea and run
off to school, often arriving late.

We rarely saw Alexander. He was at university and always studying, and we had no idea what he was doing most
of the time. He had two friends, Leonid and Ivan, brothers
who studied with him in the school of mathematics. They
were very rich orphans whose parents' estate was managed
by V. P. Malyshev, the inspector of public schools. Their

property at 1 Meshchansky Street was an expansive estate with a large park and many lilac bushes. The brothers lived in their parents' mansion and V. P. Malyshev lived in the guesthouse outside the gates. When Leonid and Ivan became legal adults, they took control of the estate and began to squander their money on drinking sprees and women of a certain reputation. Alexander kept them company occasionally and even tried to introduce our humble and unpretentious brother Ivan to their revels. However, Ivan kept his distance and conducted himself with such dignity that he never fit in. Malyshev, who was no doubt upset about the way the parents' money was being put to use, noticed Ivan's good behavior and took a shine to him.

Due to our limited circumstances, Ivan could not afford to continue his studies and was preparing to go teach in the country when Malyshev suggested that Ivan take the parochial teacher exam. Having passed the simple exam in Zvenigorod, Ivan was soon assigned by Malyshev to Voskresensk, a small town in Moscow province—which is why he wasn't mentioned among the residents of our apartment at the Savitsky house.

Anton's Taganrog scholarship arrived quarterly, in a lump sum. It did not do much to ease his circumstances, because the minute it arrived he had to use it to settle debts, buy an overcoat, pay the tuition, and so forth. The hundred rubles were always gone within a day. The very first time he received the scholarship money I remember him buying a pile of comic magazines, including a copy of *Dragonfly*.[7] At some point, he apparently submitted a piece he wrote to *Dragonfly* and started buying it every week, anxiously awaiting a response in the magazine's letters section. It was in the winter and I can still recall how Anton's frozen fingers would leaf clumsily through the pages of the latest issue he had just picked up on his way home from the university. Finally an answer came: "Not bad at all, our blessings for future cooperation." At last, in March of 1880, the tenth issue of *Dragonfly* printed Anton's first piece. It was the beginning of his professional literary life.

The piece, "A Letter to a Learned Neighbor," was actually the same monologue he had performed for us at home. He always performed it for guests, playing the part of a shabby professor delivering a public lecture on his discoveries. Our whole family was overjoyed about the publication of Anton's first piece, and the joy was doubled for me because my translation of a poem by the German poet Friedrich Rückert had also just been published in *Light and Shadows.* I received one ruble and twenty kopecks as payment.

As I mentioned earlier, my brother Nikolay was studying fine arts on Myasnitskaya Street, in the College of Painting, Sculpture, and Architecture. In one of his evening classes, he befriended a fellow student, K. I. Makarov, who would walk to the college from his house in the remote Lefortovo District. Makarov was already a drawing instructor at the Third Military School, but he wanted to become a serious artist and dreamt of retiring from the military and dedicating himself entirely to art. Makarov became a frequent guest and grew to love our family. We would often make the long walk to Lefortovo to visit him. Makarov eventually did retire from the military and went to Saint Petersburg to apply to the Academy of the Arts, but he died from typhoid in the autumn.

In Lefortovo we met and befriended M. M. Dyukovsky, another instructor at the Third Military School. He loved arts, was highly receptive to all things artistic, and became a passionate admirer of my brothers Nikolay and Anton. He cherished each and every line Anton wrote and treasured every single piece of scrap paper with Nikolay's drawings on it, preserving them as carefully as if they were worthy of a museum. When Nikolay was beginning a large painting like *Strolling in Sokolniky* or *Messalina,* Dyukovsky would let him use his room on campus as a studio; my brother's easels usually took up the entire room. He was also a willing and patient model for the paintings, and would even dress as a woman when Nikolay needed to work on the folds of a dress. We got a laugh out of seeing this young, bearded man dressed like a woman. Nikolay immortalized him as the young man in the forefront carrying a bouquet in *Strolling in Sokolniky.* People sometimes think that this is my brother Anton, but they are incorrect.

We liked visiting Dyukovsky, although the walk from Grachiovka to Lefortovo was no small feat, and Anton and I would make the trek in spite of biting frost. It was especially scary for us to walk across the Yauzky Bridge, because the river never froze and would rush loudly past the dismal wastelands by the bridge. Anton never forgot that bridge, even after he became a well-known writer. We went for

Dyukovsky's hospitality and for his large collection of illustrated magazines that he either subscribed to or borrowed from the school's library. Sometimes we would take
the magazines home but carrying them in the freezing cold
was difficult, since we needed to be able to rub our fingers,
warm our ears with our hands, and stomp our numb feet.

After a disagreement with his supervisors at the military school, Dyukovsky got a new job at the Bourgeois College at the other end of Moscow. It was on Kaluzhsky
Street, and he worked there as a house manager in exchange for room and board. We would visit him there, too,
and he once again let Nikolay transform his apartment into
a studio.

What's more, Dyukovsky nearly became part of our
family at one point. My Mother had a cousin in Shuya who
had married N. A. Zakoryukin, the local mayor. Mayor Zakoryukin had a daughter from his first marriage who was
married to a man named I. I. Lyadov. The daughter died
and left Lyadov with a daughter, Yulinka, who was taken in
by her grandparents after her mother's death. When
Yulinka turned eighteen, the plan was for her to marry
Dyukovsky, since she was well mannered and had a dowry
of about 40,000 rubles. Dyukovsky embraced the plan
and went with Nikolay to Shuya to introduce himself to
the old Zakoryukins. Some biographers assert that
Dyukovsky went there with Anton rather than Nikolay,
but that is incorrect.

Although the planned marriage never came to pass, it
introduced Nikolay and Anton to Lyadov, the girl's father,

and his brother-in-law, F. I. Gundobin, which led to a fast friendship and their frequent visits to Moscow. Since they were well off, they would take my brothers to restaurants, including the then-infamous Salon des Variétés ("The Salty Den"), and brothels. There the Shuya men's mercantile swagger was on full display, prompting Anton to give Gundobin the nickname "Mukhtar," which stayed with him into old age. Both men inspired characters in several of Anton's stories. In the penultimate paragraph in Chekhov's 1881 story "Salon des Variétés," published in *Spectator*'s eleventh issue, you can find Lyadov and Mukhtar along with my callow brothers—all four are mentioned under their real names.

While Anton was contributing pieces to *Dragonfly,* my eldest brother Alexander was writing occasionally for another magazine called *Alarm Clock,* where one of his stories, "Carl and Emilia," earned him some attention. Meanwhile, the editors at *Dragonfly* had begun sending Anton's articles back with rather acerbic responses. After he had published about a dozen articles in *Dragonfly,* a response appeared in the letters section that said, "Not in bloom yet, but withering already. What a pity. One really shouldn't write without turning a critical eye on oneself."

Anton was hurt and began looking around for another magazine to write for. He did not like *Alarm Clock* or *Entertainment* much, but he couldn't find a publication that seemed much better. I believe that it was around this time that a group of Moscow writers decided to publish a new literary almanac called *Imp* and approached Anton and Nikolay to write and illustrate for it. Nikolay enthusiastically took to working on the illustrations along with the artist A. S. Yanov. Anton intended to write something but never got around to it, so *Imp* was published without his material and Anton did not make any money. Another opportunity soon presented itself, however, in the form of the magazine *Spectator*. In a later incarnation, the magazine could be said to have become fully "Chekhovian," since all the literary and artistic production was handled by my three brothers: Alexander, Anton, and Nikolay, with Alexander in charge of the administrative duties. Every day after school I would go to their office on Strastnoy Boulevard in the Vasiliev building near Tverskaya.

V. V. Davydov was the founder of *Spectator*. He ran a small printing press and his wife had a boutique. He was also a very enthusiastic photographer. No matter his plans, they were always grand and sure to be enormous. Whenever he got excited about something, he would gesture so frenetically and speak with so much passion that his spittle would fly in all directions. He also whistled while he spoke, so his speech often sounded like this: "Oh boy, will I have (whistle!) this and that! . . . Oh boy (whistle!), and then I will open another (whistle!) and it will be so big (whistle!) that the devil only knows (whistle)!"

At the time, all illustrated magazines in Moscow were still printed lithographically—zincography was only beginning to come into use. Only *Dragonfly*, in Saint Petersburg, used zinc clichés, because it was published by professional zincographer German Kornfeld. But Davydov seized on zincography with a passion and, to quote Anton, "started ruining his artists' drawings." Davydov built himself a very primitive zincography shop, consisting of three boxes sealed with tar and filled with nitric acid (whose vapors Davydov inhaled all day long) and a roller with black dye, on which he rolled the drawings transferred onto zinc. Without a kopeck to his name and only this rudimentary equipment, he launched the *Spectator*. The magazine was supposed to come out three times a week (whistle!), eclipse every other Moscow publication (whistle!), and cost only three rubles a year. Its inaugural issue was planned to attract no less than 20,000 subscribers (whistle!).

Davydov's undertaking may have had financial help from O. I. Seletsky, who was employed in a Moscow bank, and from Ozeretsky, an assistant solicitor. Those two were always loafing around the office with my brothers and the provincial actor Struzhkin. Struzhkin wrote verses under the pen name "Awl," and Alexander always joked that "unfortunately this particular awl pricks with its blunt end." Ozeretsky was always inventing fantastic scenarios to get attention, no doubt in order to prop up his legal career. One scheme involved having either Anton or Alexander file a complaint in court alleging that Struzhkin had broken a guitar against his head. The case would be dismissed by the judge due to lack of evidence, but the plaintiff would insist and move the case to the appellate court. The other brother would then make an entertaining and humorous report in the *Spectator* on the case. However, the main reason for bringing the fake case to the court was to have the entire defense speech of "our talented and hugely promising" counsel Ozeretsky included in the report.

The *Spectator*'s office was more like a club than a real office. Staff members treated it as if it were home—they laughed, smoked, told jokes, did absolutely no work, and stayed late into the night. The caretaker, Aleksey, had to serve tea ten or more times every day. Gushchin, a mail sorter from the post office, would be there too, quietly listening to the conversations as he compiled subscribers' names. His nickname was Water-Closet, because each of his subscription reports were diligently signed "Sorter Gushchin."[8]

Another active member of the staff was the talented writer and translator Andrey Mikhailovich Dmitriev, who wrote under the pseudonym of Baron Galkin.[9] He was an editor at the *Moscow Theatrical Gazette* and, with N. Lanin, published the *Russian Courier*. He published several books and a few of his plays were produced. He was a very interesting and lively person and an engaging conversationalist. Incidentally, he once told Anton (in my presence) a story about our brother Ivan needing money so badly that he walked to the other end of the city to do dictation for the writer P. D. Boborykin, on which Anton later drew for his story "Ivan Matveevich."[10]

An amusing incident occurred in Davydov's shop. Someone was printing his own translation of *King and Bondarivna*, a novel by Polish writer Jósef Krazewsky, but had run out of money to pay for the printing and paper. So 2,000 copies sat in Davydov's storage room, tied in bundles and stacked in a corner. The caretaker Aleksey made a bed out of the books and slept on them while supposedly guarding the office (the furniture consisted only of kitchen tables and rickety stools). Since the translator had not been back in over a year, they decided to sell the books by the pound. I intervened and, displaying rare business acumen for a schoolboy, suggested that Davydov offer the book as a gift to attract subscribers to the magazine. Anton approved of the plan. Davydov was utterly delighted and, waving his arms, exclaimed, "And what do you think (whistle)? True, I only have 2,000 copies, but I'll never have more subscribers than that (whistle)! But even if I only have 2,000 subscribers—wow! Plus retail sale—wow! I will be a millionaire (whistle whistle)!" They decided to proceed with the plan and Anton even composed an advertisement, but alas— almost no one subscribed to the magazine, and the copies of *King and Bondarivna* continued to serve as Aleksey's bed.

Our brother Nikolay worked on the *Spectator*'s illustrations with enthusiasm and contributed the magazine's main vignette, as well as a number of pictures. Unfortunately, the writing in the debut issue was weak and the issue wasn't a success. Anton's first article, "Temperaments," finally appeared in Issue 5, and from that point on, my brothers were given complete control of the magazine. Nikolay drew pictures day and night, but Davydov always managed to ruin them, so they would have to be redrawn. Despite Anton's prodigious contributions, the magazine simply did not take off. They found themselves struggling to publish three issues a week, so it ran late a few times, and its readership dwindled. In an effort to save face, Davydov printed an editorial note saying that the artist N. P. Chekhov was almost blind with an eye ailment, so the magazine's publication had to be temporarily suspended. The subscribers responded with letters to the effect that although they wished the artist a quick recovery, they felt the magazine could not abandon its commitments.

While the *Spectator* was still publishing, the famous actress Sarah Bernhardt came to Moscow. Her tour gave my brothers rich material, and one issue's centerfold featured Nikolay's outstanding illustration of the Bolshoy Theater during a Bernhardt performance.

As far as I can remember, Anton only worked at the *Spectator* for a year and was not part of the magazine's later revival. He wrote a remarkably funny satire about the *Spectator* titled "Temple of Glory," and handed the manuscript to V. V. Davydov, but I do not know what happened to it. The *Spectator*'s publication spurred on other magazines in Moscow. In fact, *Alarm Clock,* threatened by the competition, even started printing its cover in gold ink. Anton and Nikolay both ended up at *Alarm Clock* after the *Spectator*'s demise.

IV

THE MOSCOW
LITERARY
MAGAZINES

ALARM CLOCK'S OFFICES WERE LOCATED IN THE MICHINER building in Leontievsky Alley. L. N. Utkina was the publisher and A. D. Kurepin[1] was the editor at the magazine. Kurepin, aside from his work at *Alarm Clock,* wrote a satirical column about life in Moscow for *New Time.* He would answer every question with another question: "Why? But why?" Another important figure at *Alarm Clock* was Nikolay Petrovich Kicheev.[2] Kicheev, too, wrote satirical columns for other magazines—first *Voice* and then *News.* He was also a big theatergoer who wrote reviews and dabbled at playwriting.

Kicheev once gave me a chance to earn some money by making four copies of *The War with the German,* a play he had coauthored with F. F. Popudoglo. It was a tedious play and closed the day after it opened, but Kicheev did pay me for my work—a whole twenty-five rubles—which I planned to use for my tuition. My brothers, however, got hold of the money and quickly spent it. When the time came to pay my tuition, the school inspector told me to either have the money or not to bother coming back the next day. Nikolay and Anton went knocking on various magazines' doors, pleading for their royalties. It was very late by the time they returned. Waking me, they solemnly handed over a bundle so heavy that I almost dropped it. My twenty-five rubles were there—entirely in silver dimes. It turned out that my brothers had stayed in one of the offices until the newsboys selling magazines for ten kopecks apiece came back from the streets. The next morning I lugged the money to school in my satchel, seriously puzzling the inspector by paying the entire fee in dimes. He kept asking me where I got them but I just mumbled something about getting them from my parents.

Sweet and well-mannered, Kicheev was also an enjoyable and very interesting conversationalist. I remember well the wonderful smell of cologne that would emanate from him when he visited my brothers, and whenever I came to see him at *Alarm Clock,* he would entertain me with tea so strong and black as tar that I only drank it to be polite. For the job of copying the play I was recommended to him by Anton. I had also copied a long drama of his— not once but twice—which similarly never saw the light of day. I do not recall the title of Anton's play, but it was something banal, involving horse thieves, gunshots, and a woman throwing herself under a moving train. Still, I remember feeling caught up in the action while copying it, my heart sinking to the pit of my stomach from empathy and worry. At the time, Anton was a second-year university student and he had taken the play to M. N. Ermolova[3] to read—he wanted her to produce it for her benefit performance. But she returned the play and my hard work turned out to be for nothing. It was later published by the Central Archive.

Since I mentioned Kicheev, I also want to say a few words about his coauthor Fiodor Fedoseevich Popudoglo.[4] An old-timer who had seen it all, he was very popular in Moscow's writing circles, a man greatly respected for his honesty and decency. However, misfortune followed him and his literary work barely earned him enough to eat. He was close to Misha Evstigneev,[5] the then-famous author of little books for a general audience, whom the booksellers had exploited terribly. At every bazaar in the country, M. Evstigneev's books would be selling right off the peddler's rug. For five kopecks, you could buy any one of them, including *The Five-Ruble Smile* or *Monsieur Von-Herr* Petrushka. He wrote exclusively for those publishers who dealt with bazaar peddlers. And because his own fee for writing a book was only between fifty kopecks and a ruble fifty, the publishers' profits were huge. Misha's gift paved the way for big businesses, like Ivan D. Sytin's enormous publishing empire.[6]

Anton befriended Popudoglo after meeting him in *Alarm Clock*'s editorial offices. As he later said and even wrote in a letter, for some strange reason he began visiting Popudoglo in the evenings — "like a thief in the night" — as if he were trying to keep his visits a secret. Popudoglo was ill at that time, although not yet bedridden. From the beginning Anton correctly diagnosed him with rectal cancer and helped take care of him. When Popudoglo died, Anton lost a good friend and a stimulating conversationalist. Popudoglo bequeathed his library to Anton, but Anton still insisted on paying his widow for the books. When the huge trunk filled with books arrived, we began sorting through it only to discover that that the collection consisted entirely of common literary trash. The trunk was full of old catalogues, paperbacks by Misha Evstigneev, absolutely nothing of value, not even to a secondhand bookseller. Anton only put aside about ten books. *Songs Collected* by Rybnikov and Babikov's *Peace and Quiet* wound up at the Taganrog Library, while *The Commands for Performing the Main Functions on a Ship* gave Anton the material for Revunov-Karaulov's character in his play *The Wedding*. Everything else was simply burnt.

ć ĵ

ASIDE from my brothers, *Alarm Clock*'s contributors at the time included the artist N. Chichagov (he signed his work with the monogram "T. S."), P. A. Sergeenko[7] (his pen name was "Emil Pup"), Vladimir A. Giliarovsky,[8] whose pen name was "Uncle Giliay," and the poet L. I. Palmin.[9]

After living abroad for a long time, Sergeenko returned to Russia, began contributing to comic magazines, and finally became bogged down in the mire of Tolstoy-ism. He wrote a book about Tolstoy, but his passionate ad-miration for the subject made him think the book was more important than it actually was. As a fellow southern countryman, we were all on informal terms with him, which allowed us to appreciate why Sergeenko was con-sidered such a character. Anton told me that Sergeenko liked mocking the police, which made him the subject of a lot of anecdotes. He published two or three dramas, one of which—although written with Potapenko[10]—was un-questionably successful. In 1902, he tried to tempt me into publishing a literary journal with him and I almost agreed, but Anton talked me out of it. Sergeenko's most impor-tant role in Anton Chekhov's life was assisting in the sale of his complete works to A. F. Marks. Since this deal has been so widely talked about in the press, I won't dwell on it again here.[11]

Palmin was hunched-over and pockmarked, and had a speech impediment that left him unable to pronounce the letter "r" properly. His sloppy dressing always inspired pity. But Palmin also possessed a noble and compassionate heart, and an incredible soft spot for animals. Whenever he came to visit us, five or six dogs would burst through the door with him: one without a leg, another without an eye, yet another with a bloody and scabby back. He picked them up on his way home and gave them all refuge. He was at once highly gifted and completely downtrodden. In his early years, he had contributed to *Reading Library* and *Spark*. Although he was a wonderful poet with an elegant style, his unfortunate appetite for beer (yes, beer, not wine) led to his ultimate downfall. He was not yet an old man when we knew him, but he already walked with a stoop. He tended to live in back alleys with terrible names, so it was frightening even to go visit him. He lived with an uneducated shrew named Avdotia; Anton nicknamed her "Fefela," which stuck with her forever. She loved to drink, too, and in order to get her share, she would incite Palmin: "Liodor Ivanovich, isn't it time for your beer?"

Palmin spoke several foreign languages, translated classical literature, and wrote delightful verses. Anton once asked him to send over the new charter of some society or other. Palmin accompanied it with a special poem, of which I remember only a few lines:

> *My colleague, dearest Antosha,*
> *Just slightly jaded, though no martyr,*
> *My hair ruffled to contortion—*
> *I'm sending you the promised charter.*
> *Seeing Kalashnikov's good ale*
> *Playfully glint and never stale,*
> *I feel the bottom of this grail*
> *Inspires me to raise my tail.*
> *Just like the builder needs his lime*
> *We poets hunger for the rhyme . . .*

Quite by accident, Palmin played a very important role in Anton's literary career. Palmin occasionally wrote verses for *Fragments,* a comic magazine published by the famous humorist N. A. Leikin in Saint Petersburg.[12] On a visit to Moscow, Leikin took Palmin to dinner at the Testov restaurant and on their way back, their cab happened to pass my brothers Nikolay and Anton in the street. Pointing at them, Palmin told Leikin: "Those are two talented brothers: one is an artist and the other is a writer; both work at local comic magazines." Leikin stopped the cab and Palmin called my brothers over. He introduced them to Leikin, who immediately offered Anton work at *Fragments*. This was how Anton's literary career shifted from Moscow to St. Petersburg, where his fame began to take off.

V. A. Giliarovsky deserves further introduction. Once, early in our Moscow life, Anton came home and said, "Mom, tomorrow Giliarovsky is coming to visit me. It would be good to offer him something special." The next day happened to be Sunday, and Mother baked cabbage pie and readied some vodka. Giliarovsky was still a young man at the time and when he arrived, *joie de vivre* was literally bursting out of him. He was of average height, but powerfully built and sporting tall hunting boots. Instantly on a first-name basis with everyone, he offered his steely biceps to feel, rolled a coin into a tube, twisted a teaspoon into a screw, let everyone smell his tobacco, did several amazing tricks with cards, told many risqué jokes, and finally departed, leaving a pretty good impression in his wake. From then on, he visited regularly, always bringing his own special liveliness. We learned that he wrote poetry (his favorite poetic themes were the Mother Volga River, river pirates, and the violent and carefree lifestyle of the Cossacks) in addition to reporting for the adventure section of the *Russian Bulletin*. He was quite an exceptional reporter.

Giliarovsky knew how to get himself introduced to practically anyone in power. It seemed like everyone knew him and he knew everyone—there was nowhere he wasn't welcome. Characteristically, he treated everybody—from counts and princes to janitors and rank-and-file policemen—with the same familiarity. He could get in anywhere, always getting backstage, never paying for a train ticket, etc. He was at home in both the prim English Club and in the darkest slums of Khitrov Market. When my fur coat was stolen, I went straight to Giliarovsky, who took me to the areas solely inhabited by murderers and rogues to find it. When the Moscow Art Theater was working on Gorky's play *The Lower Depths,* it was Giliarovsky who introduced the actors to the city's underbelly. He knew every joke and no matter how much he drank, he never got drunk. He also possessed an amazing physical strength that he liked to show off. He could pet the fiercest chained dogs, pull trees out of the ground, and stop a horse from pulling a carriage just by grabbing the back wheel. There was a dynamometer for the public to measure its strength in the Hermitage Garden; while testing his strength, Giliarovsky rocked the machine off its foundation.

In May of 1885, I finished school and started my final exams. Anton, Masha, and Mother did not want to wait for me and headed off to spend the summer in Babkino, leaving me alone in the apartment. As a prospective university student, I was permitted to dine in the student cafeteria, so I would walk from Sretenka to Dolgorukovsky Alley to eat there every day. They charged only twenty-eight kopecks, but the food was so bad and the portions so small that I was always hungry again by the time I got home.

One day while crossing Bolshaya Dmitrovka on my way home from the cafeteria, I heard someone calling my name: "Hey Misha, where are you off to?" It was Giliarovsky. He was in a cab on his way to some assignment. I approached and said I was going home. "Get in," he said, "I'll give you a lift." I was only too glad to comply. But after a few minutes, Giliarovsky suddenly remembered that he needed to see Lentovsky at the Hermitage Theater. So instead of going home, I found myself at a musical comedy in Samotek. We got there just in time for the five o'clock show. "Just sit here," said Giliarovsky when we walked into the theater, "I'll be right back."

The curtain rose and the chorus appeared. Giliarovsky still was not back by the time the chorus had finished muddling its way through the opening number. A student was not allowed to attend these kinds of theaters and I was starting to get nervous. Suddenly an usher appeared and asked for my ticket. Of course, I did not have one, so he grabbed me by the sleeve and started pulling me toward the exit. Luckily Giliarovsky emerged out of nowhere at that very moment. "What's the matter? What's going on?" he said. "Well, they are asking for my ticket," I mumbled. "Ah, you mean his ticket?" Giliarovsky asked. "Of course, my dear, here's his ticket," he said, tearing off a small piece of newspaper and handing it to the usher. The usher grinned and let us both back in.

But sitting still was not for Giliarovsky. "Let's go, I don't have time," he said and we walked out of the Hermitage. "I think I wanted to give you a lift home," he remembered, "so where is our cab?" He looked around and saw our cab down at the corner—a policeman must not have let it stay at the entrance—with the cabbie peacefully asleep in his seat. Approaching the cab, Giliarovsky jolted the coach-box so hard that the cabbie tipped over and almost fell off. "Fool, damn you! Drooling here! You can sleep later!" The cabbie woke up and we got moving.

On the corner of Sadovaya, where we should have made a turn to go to Sretenka, Giliarovsky suddenly remembered that he needed to be at Riazansky station! So we made our way there, or rather his way there, since I was just a helpless passenger at that point. When we reached the station, he paid the driver, sent him off, and took me inside. Walking through the station, Giliarovsky managed to shake hands and chitchat with at least a dozen friends. Suddenly he dashed toward a departing train, leaving me behind. The train slowly began moving with Giliarovsky still standing in the door. "Farewell Mishenka!" he yelled to me as I started running along the moving car. "Let's shake hands!" he said and I extended my hand to him. He grabbed it so forcefully that I was lifted into the air. An instant later, he had pulled me onto the train and set me down next to him.

So there I was, next to Giliarovsky, going somewhere on a train. I had no idea where the mighty man was taking me and I was worried because I did not have a single kopeck on me. We entered the car and sat down. Giliarovsky pulled out a bunch of newspapers and started reading. I tried to look offended. Finally, I said, "Vladimir Aleksee-vich, where are you taking me?" He replied, without even lifting his eyes off the paper, "Do you really care?"

The train conductor came through and began inspecting passengers' tickets. I felt as if I were about to be strip-searched. I did not have a ticket or money, and my gut was telling me that I would be in big trouble. "Your tickets, please!" barked the conductor. Without lifting his eyes off the paper, Giliarovsky tore off two little scraps, just as he had done at the theater, and offered them to the conductor. The conductor took the scraps, very respectfully punched them, handed them back to Giliarovsky, and proceeded to the next seat. What a relief! By then, I was beginning to feel amused by the whole adventure.

We got off the train in Lubertsy or Malakhovka, I think, and began walking through a thick forest. I had not been out of the city for a whole year, and it was a real pleasure to breathe in the rich scent of pines and young birch trees, to see the twilight, and to feel our feet sinking in the sand! We had been walking for a couple of miles when I spotted a small village full of warmly glowing windows and heard distant dog barking. We entered the front yard of one little house and Giliarovsky knocked on the window. A woman with a child came out of the house. "Manya," he said to her, "I brought you a guest."

We went inside. The only pieces of furniture were a large table that stood in the middle of the room and benches that lined the walls; a typical arrangement for a peasant hut. Everything was as clean as if it had been scrubbed and washed just before we came. "Well, hello Manya! Hello Alioshka!" Giliarovsky kissed both of them and introduced me to the woman. She was his wife, Maria Ivanovna, and the two-year-old was their son. "He already lifts weights!" bragged Giliarovsky. He stood the child on the table and gave him two dumbbells. The boy puffed up his cheeks and lifted one off the table. I was horrified, worried the child would drop it on his feet. But his father was beaming with pride saying, "Here! Good boy!"

That was how I unexpectedly showed up at Giliarovsky's summer retreat in Kraskovo. I spent that night and the next day there, too, as Maria Ivanovna would not let me return to Moscow. I liked being there so much that I returned between all of my exams.

During one of my visits to Kraskovo, Giliarovsky brought a huge black horse from Moscow. He had bought it from some soldiers for only twenty-five rubles. The horse had been so cheap because it was impossible to tame and would bite, buck, and toss its rider. But Giliarovsky did not seem in the least dismayed. Confident that he could break the horse through his own physical strength, he told me, "Just wait, very soon you'll see me ride him to Moscow and back." He took the horse out to the shed and all we could hear was kicking and neighing. Giliarovsky was screaming at the horse and trying to break him. When he closed the shed door behind him Maria Ivanovna and I were afraid that the horse would kill him. Giliarovsky and the horse made such a racket in that small shed that one would have thought they were having a fistfight. When Giliarovsky returned from his Bucefalus, he was covered in sweat and his hands were covered in blood. But he would not admit that the horse had bit him and said jauntily: "See, I smacked this swine in the mouth so hard that I hurt my knuckles." Finally, Giliarovsky lost hope and gave him away to a peasant who took the horse to the slaughterhouse.

Giliarovsky maintained a close friendship with Anton until my brother's death and was very affectionate with all of us. In the 1890s he would visit us in Melikhovo and continued to amaze us with his demonstrations of strength. Once, he put us all in one cart and, pulling it like a horse, gave us a ride around the estate. This is what Anton wrote to Suvorin about one such visit: "Giliarovsky was here. God only knows what he did! He wore out all my horses, climbed trees, intimidated the dogs, and broke logs to show his strength."[13]

I cannot recall a time when Giliarovsky, with his jokes and pranks, did not act like a teenager. I remember one episode in particular when he almost got us into serious trouble. There was a tailor named Belousov who lived in Moscow, in Zariadie. He had a son, Ivan Alekseevich, who later became a well-known poet, translator, and member of the Society of Friends of Russian Literature. At that time though, he was still a bashful tailor who wrote occasional poems. Belousov decided to marry off his darling son. So they rented a restaurant in the Zamoskvorechie District, hired musicians, and invited both friends and strangers. I think there were probably more than a hundred guests there. Belousov had made clothes for some of the teachers at the Bourgeois College, where Ivan worked. He had also made clothes for me, so he invited all the Chekhov brothers to the wedding. However, only three of us went— Anton, Ivan, and I—with Giliarovsky tagging along.

At the wedding, we met the groom's friend and best man, Nikolay Dmitrievich Teleshov.[14] A young and handsome fellow, he danced all night long while holding on to his top hat. He went on to become a well-known writer and his writing career was later celebrated by the Writers' Union.[15]

It was dawn and the city was beginning to stir by the time we made our way home from the wedding. There were still suspicious characters out but a few shops and taverns had opened early to serve the cab drivers. Anton, Ivan, Giliarovsky, Teleshov, and I were all very thirsty, so passing by one tavern, Anton said, "Gentlemen, let's have some tea." So the five of us, dressed in coattails, sat down at a filthy table inside. Everyone else there had just woken up. Some cabbies were saying their morning prayers and others were drinking tea. We felt out of place and a few people circled our table to have a better look at us. Giliarovsky meanwhile went on cracking jokes using his usual choice words. Anton and Teleshov talked about literature. Then one of the cabbies said: "They look like gentlemen but behave like ____."

Of course, he was right, but Giliarovsky felt like fooling around. He jumped up, got close to the cabbie's face, and said: "Wait, wait—didn't I escape from jail with you?" That comment was not appreciated! The other cabbies also jumped up but did not know what to do—should they grab Giliarovsky and drag him to the police? Should they drag their own friend to the police? Or should they just try to calm everyone down? The incident was soon settled, however. Giliarovsky cracked another joke, treated the cabbies to some snuff tobacco, and the moralist among them quietly slipped away. We made our exit. I wonder if Teleshov even remembers that episode. He was so engaged in his conversation with Anton that he probably did not even notice what had happened.

In 1882, during the time that Anton was contributing to *Alarm Clock,* he was also working for I. I. Klang. Klang was a lithographer, but I assume he didn't make a living at it since he also drew rather mediocre caricatures for minor magazines. To be fair, all the illustrated magazines in Moscow at that time were minor. I suppose he decided to start publishing a thick, illustrated art magazine in 1882 in order to improve his financial situation and keep his lithographic shop open. The magazine was called *Moscow* and all of the illustrations in it were supposed to be in color. For the time, it was a gutsy and original undertaking. A number of artists were recruited—my brother Nikolay, N. Bogatev, and I. Levitan among them—and Anton was invited to contribute to the literature section. Klang worked very hard to make the first issues impressive, and to the undiscerning eye the magazine would have indeed seemed artsy. Some of the colored illustrations were really very good. Nikolay printed a lithograph of his large painting *Strolling in Sokolniky* in the magazine. He also printed "Tipsy," a funny caricature inspired by our elder brother Alexander, who was drinking a lot at that time. Contrary to what was suggested in the press, the caricature was not based on Anton.

For some reason, Anton's first contribution to *Moscow* was a theater review, not a story. But then taking pity on the magazine, he very generously gave them his novella *Cape Green*,[16] complete with excellent illustrations by Nikolay. But the magazine's limited means and the public's indifference prevented *Moscow* from taking off. For some reason Klang decided to rename it *Wave,* but that did not help either, and the business eventually closed. I went to the office many times trying to collect Anton's royalties but as soon as I showed up, the publisher would slip out through the back door.

I had to collect my brother's royalties quite often, actually. He was always busy and I was his debt collector of choice. He even issued me a fake power of attorney that looked like this:

Certificate

Issued to Mikhail Pavlovich Chekhov, student of the Moscow Imperial University, of Christian Orthodox faith; this certifies that he has been my brother since 1865 and is authorized by me to receive money from any and all literary offices with which I have collaborated. The signature and seal below bear witness.

Moscow, day 15 of the month of January, 1886.

Doctor A. Chekhov

I used to get Anton's royalties from *The News of the Day* with this kind of certificate. Oh, those days were so hard for me! Anton was supposed to receive three rubles a week for his novel *The Shooting Party*,[17] which was published in *The News of the Day* in 1884. I would sit in that office and wait and wait and wait for the newsboys to return with the daily receipts. The publisher would always ask me, "What exactly are you waiting for?" "Well, I'm here to get Anton's three rubles." He would reply, "I don't have it! Would you like a theater ticket or maybe a new pair of pants? Why don't you go to Arontrikher the tailor and get yourself a pair of pants on my account?"

I don't remember the location of *The News of the Day*'s office now, I think it was somewhere on Tverskaya, near Gazetny Alley. But the entire office was just one room. They received subscribers there and the staff would all talk at the same time, so the office was very noisy. They also had a grand piano on which Lipskerov's niece—or maybe it was his sister-in-law—practiced scales. Her music teacher would tower over her and keep time by stomping her foot and chanting, "one-two-three-four—one-two-three-four." I had to wait in the middle of all that for hours and hours just to collect the three rubles. I wanted to go home so much!

The News of the Day, or as Anton called it, "the noose of the day," was published by Abram Yakovlevich Lipskerov. Before he started publishing the newspaper he was one of the best, if not the best, stenographer, and worked recording hearings in the district court. F. N. Plevako, the famous defense attorney who was at that point still trying to build up his reputation, would take him along to the provincial courts. Lipskerov would record Plevako's speeches and they would subsequently appear word for word in the Moscow papers.

Their business soon improved, however. Rumor spread that his paper was predicting rather precisely which horse would win the upcoming race. A few successes at the track worked their magic and the newspaper was soon thriving. *The News of the Day* acquired its own building—practically a palace—near Krasnye Vorota, and thoroughbred horses pulled the publisher's new carriage.

❧   ❧

ANTON's novel *The Shooting Party* was not his first long piece. He had previously published a novel called *Unnecessary Victory*[18] in *Alarm Clock,* which he had written quite by accident. He had made a bet with Kurepin, *Alarm*

Clock's editor, that he could write a novel as good as those that were translated into Russian. Kurepin did not believe it. The bet dictated that Anton would write and publish the novel in installments in the magazine, while Kurepin reserved the right to stop publishing it at any time. The novel turned out to be so engaging and popular that it was published in its entirety. As I remember, people even wrote in asking whether the novel was written by Mavr Iokai or Friedrich von Spielhagen.[19]

My brothers Nikolay and Anton also worked for the magazines *Light and Shadows* and *Worldly Sense*. The publisher of both, N. L. Pushkariov,[20] was a highly intelligent and well-educated man. He had been very popular as a satirical poet in the vein of Nekrasov,[21] and his denunciatory poems like "Nasty, Vile, Indecent," "Well, It's All Right," or "Three Nannies of Different Nations and Natures" were recited on every stage. Only the rare provincial actor did not include Pushkariov's poems in his repertoire, so they were heard all over the country. But although the poems were on everybody's lips, very few knew who wrote them. Pushkariov was also a playwright whose play *Ksenia and Lzhedimitry* was produced in various theaters.

The highly enterprising and inventive Pushkariov owned a house on Brigadirsky Street, where he had his printing press, his lithographic shop, his editorial office, and a rather sizable apartment. In the beginning, he published the weekly *Moscow Review*, which printed Shklarevsky's *The Morning after the Ball, or Murder in the Chinese Baths,* a crime novel based on a recent sensational court case that was on everybody's mind in Moscow. The comic *Light and Shadows* came next, which he published alongside the *Moscow Review,* by then renamed *Worldly Sense.*

Light and Shadows addressed the social and political events of the day with great perceptiveness and honesty, which twice led to it being censored. The first time it was shut down for six months; the second time it was barred from retail sale for an extended period of time. Of course, this seriously undermined the magazine's financial stability. But Pushkariov had earned the public's support—especially when, after Alexander II's assassination on March 1, 1881, he printed a cartoon depicting the gallows with the caption, "Our solution to vital issues."

Rather than lose heart, Pushkariov just started another publication—*The European Library.* It was a substantial weekly journal that included a complete translation of a novel by a foreign author in each issue. To its credit, *The European Library* was the first to introduce Russian readers to writers like Hector Malot, Karl Emil Franzos, Alphonse Daudet, Terrier, Émile Zola, and Pierre Loti. Considering his limited finances, it was astonishing how many books Pushkariov was able to publish. *The European Library* was around for about a year and a half, I think. The subscribers barely had time to read such a huge number of books. Twelve or so issues would have been plenty, as opposed to fifty.

Worldly Sense was remembered fondly for having published Samuel Taylor Coleridge's "Rime of the Ancient

Mariner," with wonderful illustrations by Gustave Doré. Anton published his novel *Late-Blooming Flowers*[22] in *Worldly Sense* and Nikolay published a number of drawings and cartoons in *Light and Shadows. Light and Shadows* also published some of my drawings under Nikolay's name as well as my puzzles, offering a prize for the winner. *The European Library* had planned to publish my translation from the German of Moritz Hartmann, but "for reasons beyond editorial control" the manuscript was rejected by the censor. Just imagine, a simple student like me translating such pernicious material that it could not even pass the censor! Had my school administrators known, they would have been very alarmed.

In general, that period was a very promising one for my writing. I wrote a novel and took it to *The A. Gatsuk Newspaper,* where it would have been published had not that simple paper been closed down. I read a lot of social literature, was getting paid for my magazine work, and I was even able to buy myself a pocket watch. To have a watch and read reprehensible books by writers like Pierre-Joseph Proudhon seemed like the height of political free-thinking and nonconformism for a schoolboy. Anton never passed up a chance to make fun of me. He would say, "Look at him, he knows Gatsuk, he disagrees with Proudhon, and he flaunts a watch!" Anton did not yet own a pocket watch.

We were all fascinated by the new advances in science, art, and literature—especially Pushkariov. When a famous hypnotist named German was prohibited from conducting a public séance, Pushkariov decided to host the séance in his home. He invited professors and representatives of the Moscow press and asked my brothers to bring the famous Professor Ostroumov.[23]

The hypnotist astonished the guests and left even the professors baffled. He put a person into a trance, and even stopped his blood from circulating. The hypnotized person's veins were punctured in several places, but no blood appeared. The strangest trick, which stymied Professor Ostroumov, was when the hypnotist stopped his subject's heart. The subject's brain still functioned and he could see, smell, hear, and even answer questions. How could this man's brain continue to function while his heart and lungs were completely paralyzed? As Ostroumov loudly exclaimed, "There's the rub!"

It was a fearful sight when the hypnotist made the man's body stiff as a wooden log or a stone. He placed the back of his head on one chair and his heels on another, while three adults sat on him as they would on a bench. Meanwhile, the subject remained completely oblivious and was surprised when, upon being awoken, he was told what he had just experienced. In those days it was all very new and considered so inexplicable that even learned professors didn't know what to make of it.

Widely gifted man that he was, Pushkariov usually tired of his various projects quickly. Or perhaps the range of his interests was so broad that he could never concentrate on only one thing. He was a passionate fisher who invented an automatic reel for his fishing pole, for which he never received credit. He opened a photography shop on Lubyanka, but then decided to dedicate himself entirely to another of his inventions, the "Pushkariov candle." It became the most common petroleum burner used internationally, usually by housewives to make coffee or curl their hair. Unfortunately, the international rights were sold for a song, and this fact, together with his publishing failures, soon led to Pushkariov's financial ruin. It was said that he died in abject poverty.

I would like to say a few words here about *Cricket,* another magazine to which Anton contributed. Modeled on French magazines of the day, it was published by the two Verner brothers—Evgeny and Mikhail. Young, vivacious, and full of energy, they had lived abroad for a long time and returned to Russia to do business "the right way." They also founded the magazine *Around the World,* which introduced the reading public to the writings of Louis Henri Boussenard, Robert Louis Stevenson, Henry Rider Haggard, and others. A very engaging magazine for its time, every student subscribed to it. Because business was booming, they purchased a huge printing plant in Arbat and began publishing two more magazines: the comic *Cricket* and one for children, *Children's Friend.*

While they managed to grab readers' attention with *Around the World,* the brothers did not have the same success with the new ventures. *Cricket*'s exterior was quite original, and the brothers deserve credit for introducing stenciled watercolors to Russia. But *Cricket*'s content was rather lifeless, and as for *Children's Friend,* to which I also contributed, it was just plain boring. Children didn't like it and it could not even compete with the poorly published *Children's Leisure.* Nonetheless, whenever you visited the Verners' printing plant, you would find the machines roaring, and the brothers working right there on the floor in their blue smocks.

They also published books, including a collection of Anton's short stories called *Innocent Talks,* with a cover illustration by Nikolay. Without fail, their publications were elegant and original, and under different circumstances they could have no doubt been very successful. Neither brother shied away from even the most menial tasks, but like true Europeans, when they were off work, they dressed in the most exquisite and fashionable clothes. Anton Pavlovich made fun of them in "Moscow Life Fragments," published in Leikin's magazine. He wrote, "Do you think publishing magazines is easy? Not as easy as wearing fancy vests with painted horses." Unaware that Anton was the author, the Verners complained to him that someone "was making fun at their expense."

The Verners eventually went bankrupt. *Around the World* was acquired by I. D. Sytin, and *Cricket* and *Children's Friend* simply disappeared. I think it was then that both Verner brothers moved abroad again.

V

THE YOUNG
DOCTOR

As I mentioned, my middle brother Ivan passed
the teacher's exam in 1880 and was assigned to Voskresensk, a backwater town in the Moscow province. Less
than a mile from the town was a famous monastery called
New Jerusalem, which had been founded by Patriarch
Nikon so that Russian pilgrims would not have to travel all
the way to Palestine to pay homage to the so-called sacred
places. An exact replica of the Jerusalem Temple in Palestine, New Jerusalem, had its own Calvary, Lord's Tomb
Chapel, Gethsemane Garden, Kidron Stream, and even
two biblical mountains, Tabor and Hermon.

In those days, Voskresensk was still a tiny town and my
brother was put in charge of its sole parochial school. The
school's trustee, the famous textile manufacturer Tsurikov,
spared no expense to make Ivan Pavlovich feel comfortable. Suddenly my brother found himself living in a large,

well-furnished apartment big enough for a whole family. Compared to the rest of us Chekhovs, living in cramped poverty in Moscow, he was immensely lucky. The minute my sister and I finished our exit exams, our Mother whisked us away to spend the summer enjoying Voskresensk's greener countryside. After Moscow, it felt like heaven on earth to my sister and me. The town was also remarkable for the mushrooms that grew on its outskirts. We Chekhovs have a true passion for mushroom picking, which made us appreciate Voskresensk that much more.

We met many interesting people in Voskresensk. Colonel B. I. Mayevsky, the man in charge of the military battery stationed in town, was lively and social. Another interesting person was P. D. Golokhvastov,[1] known for his dedicated work on the issue of provincial councils. He was a tall man with a black beard and a black mane, which sported a single gray streak that ran from his forehead all the way to the back of the head. He walked with a waddle and his head sharply bowed, so that it almost touched his chest. He was always so deep in thought that he often walked past his own house. He had to be accompanied home by a girl named Avochka, whom he later adopted as his daughter. He studied Russian history, made some important discoveries about the period called the Time of Troubles,[2] and along with the minister, N. P. Ignatiev, had plans to introduce a constitution based on old Russian provincial councils. He wrote and spoke in an archaic way, emulating the style of ancient manuscripts and coining new, cumbersome words. It was always interesting to con-

verse with him; his erudition was truly amazing and he conducted himself without any pretense. While talking, he
paced around the room constantly. His wife was the writer
Olga Andreevna, who wrote the drama *Evil to the Evil* and
the raucous vaudeville *Call Yourself a Mushroom—Jump
into the Basket.*[3]

There were two or three other interesting families in
Voskresensk, but the social life definitely centered on
Colonel Mayevsky and his family. They had charming children—Ania, Sonia, and Aliosha—whom Anton befriended
and portrayed in his short story "Children."[4] One of their
family friends was E. I. Tyshko, an officer wounded during
the Turkish War who always wore a black silk cap. In his
correspondence, Anton always referred to him as "Tyshko
in capshko." At the Mayevskys', my brother became ac-
quainted with other officers from the battery and with military life in general, which later helped him to write *The
Three Sisters.*[5] One officer of the battery, Lieutenant E. P.
Egorov, became a close friend of his and is mentioned in
Anton's novella *Cape Green*. Later, Egorov retired from
the army with a passion to "work, work, work," just like the
character Baron Tuzenbakh in *The Three Sisters*.

Anton was not with us in Voskresensk initially. He had
financial worries and stayed in Moscow to earn what money
he could from the literary magazines. So he was not able to
travel further than Sokolniky and Bogorodskoe, the summer villages close to Moscow, which he brilliantly mocked
in *Motley Stories*. The intelligentsia was very excited by the
1881 Great National Fair and the opening of the Pushkin

monument, so Anton was hardly bored in sweltering Moscow. He took advantage of these occasions to make new acquaintances, establish literary connections, and immerse himself in the world of newspapers and magazines.

One incident stands out from this period, when he received a reprimand at the National Fair that greatly upset him. That summer, there had been an accident somewhere between Chern and Bastyevo, near Kukuevka, on the Moscow-Kursk railway. A mail train filled with passengers traveling from Moscow to the south derailed and rolled off the embankment, creating a landslide and burying all of the passengers alive. Vladimir Giliarovsky was sent to cover what came to be called the Kukuevka Tragedy and reported on it in great detail.

Light and Shadows had its own booth in the fair's periodical press exhibit, which was manned by our acquaintance A. A. Ipatieva. Anton was talking to her when the news of the accident broke. Anton bought a telegram from one of the newsboys running by and became very emotional while reading it. He said loudly to Ipatieva: "Such tragedies can happen only in our swine-like Russia!" Just then, a general in a blue cap and white uniform came up to him and asked sternly, "What did you just say, young man? Say it again! I heard 'in our swine-like Russia'? What is your name? Who are you?" Anton was embarrassed and did not say anything. "All right, sir. You shall answer for this," said the general, and briskly walked away. Anton expected to be arrested and taken to Butyrki, but the general never came back.

The fair had a section devoted to music, where different companies exhibited their instruments—mostly grand pianos and organs. To attract customers, the companies invited European celebrities to play entire concerts at the exhibition booths, and one could hear some truly great artists for free. One such celebrity was the conductor P. A. Shostakovsky,[6] known for organizing philharmonic classes and concerts in Moscow, who premiered a famous rhapsody by Liszt on one of the company's grand pianos. The rhapsody so enchanted Nikolay and Anton that afterward Nikolay played it several times a day at home. Both my brothers met Shostakovsky personally and later visited him at home.

Shostakovsky was the sweetest, kindest, and most polite man, and everyone who knew him appreciated him as a great performer and adored him as a person. But when it came to making music, which he worshipped, he forgot everything and everybody and turned into a tiger ready to tear any member of the orchestra apart over the slightest mistake. If he heard one, he would immediately tap his baton and stop the orchestra. "If you, you swine," he would say to the offending musician, "spoil my ensemble again, I will kick you out!" On one such occasion, our dear friend Ivanenko, who played the flute in his orchestra, fearing that the insult was addressed to him, asked with great dignity: "I dare think, Piotr Adamovich, that these words of yours are not addressed to me, are they?" "No, no, not to you," replied the irritated Shostakovsky, "I was talking to that nincompoop!" Another incident occurred when S. M. G.

was playing percussion. Distracted and tired of waiting for the conductor to give him his measure, he hit a drum too early. Shostakovsky put his baton down and stopped the orchestra. "If you continue in this manner, I'll thrash you like a schoolboy!" Deeply offended, the drummer walked off the stage in protest. No one was ever upset with Shostakovsky outside of concerts and rehearsals, though. Everybody knew how he could be and knew that in the end he would be nice and praise everybody for the success of his orchestra.

Anton used Shostakovsky as the model for the conductor in his short story "Two Scandals."[7] That story became part of Anton's very first collection of short stories called *The Tales of Melpomene,* published in 1884. But that book had no luck.

It was printed in A. A. Levenson's shop, and all the printing costs were expected to be recouped by the sale of the first print run. The shop owners receiving the book on commission assumed the short stories were children's fairy tales and placed them in the children's section. This caused a few problems with the customers; for example, a general threw a fit at the bookshop of *New Time* because he thought they had sold him an indecent book for children. Everyone lost track of the book after that—not even Anton knew what became of it.

Another one of Anton's books from that period had similar bad luck. Anton had produced a collection of short stories, which included "Actors' Wives" and "Flying Islands,"[8] and the book was very nicely illustrated by our brother Nikolay. It got as far as being printed and bound and was only missing the cover, but for some reason it was never released, and I have no idea what happened to it.

❧   ❧

ANTON only came to Voskresensk for the summer once, just before his last year as a student. He already had a circle of friends there and they took daily walks together. Tall, dressed in a black cloak, and wearing a wide-brimmed hat, Anton took part in every stroll. And stroll they did, with a group of children running ahead. The adults would trail far behind, discussing the news of the day. There was a lot to talk about then. Aside from the books by Mikhail Saltykov-Shchedrin,[9] which everyone had read and reread, people subscribed to all of the thick journals without exception. The most popular journals to discuss on those walks were *Homeland Notes, European Herald,* and *History Herald.*[10] As a writer, Anton needed a continuous stream of new material for his stories. The life that surrounded him in Voskresensk offered him inspiration and he immersed himself in it. As a future physician, he also needed patients for his medical practice, and those, too, were in abundant supply.

There was a renowned hospital at the Chikino estate, about a mile and a half away. Situated by a big, beautiful pond, the estate had been bought by the provincial council and converted into a medical facility run by Dr. P. A. Arkhangelsky, a man well-known in medical literature and among provincial physicians. Dr. Arkhangelsky was very social and always had many young doctors studying medicine under him. We all met V. N. Sirotinin, D. S. Tauber, and M. P. Yakovlev, whose names have remained in the annals of medical science.

After a long day of work, Anton and his friends would often meet at Arkhangelsky's house (he lived alone) to drink and discuss the liberal and literary topics of the day. They would frequently speak of Shchedrin and Turgenev's novels, sing folk songs like "Show Me Such an Abode," and passionately recite Nikolay Nekrasov's poems. That was where I was called Mikhail Pavlovich for the first time, rather than Misha, and it immediately elevated my sense of self-worth. Those parties taught me invaluable political and social lessons, and my views as a man and citizen were indelibly formed there.

In 1884, Anton finished his medical coursework and came to the Chikino hospital to complete his residency. He got the plots for stories like "Escapee" and "Surgery" at that hospital, and his Voskresensk acquaintance, Postmaster Andrey Egorovich, gave him the idea for "The Government Test."[11]

There was another hospital close to Voskresensk, but it had a whole different kind of atmosphere. Affiliated with A. S. Tsurikova's textile factory in the village of Ivanovskoe, this hospital was well equipped, but not very popular. Dr. M. M. Tsvetaev was in charge. He was convinced that the patients smelled bad and would not allow them to come too close.

Incidentally, this doctor also left his mark in literature, which happened through an episode involving a Cossack named Ashinov. Ashinov called himself an ataman, or Cossack chief, but was in fact a big fraud. He hoped to discover a new continent, like Columbus did, and make it a Russian colony.

There is a strange connection between my family and Ashinov. When my Uncle Mitrofan Egorovich was young, a man came to him looking for work in Taganrog. Uncle gave him a job digging a cellar for his house. The man worked so diligently and was so well-spoken that he piqued my Uncle's interest. They started talking, and the more they talked, the more the digger captivated my Uncle. His theories ended up making a lifelong impression on my Uncle. The digger went on to become the well-known monk Paissy, and after he retired, the aforementioned Dr. M. M. Tsvetaev also became a monk.

One day, "Chief" Ashinov announced that he had discovered a new continent. The press responded with scorn, and the authorities in Saint Petersburg were skeptical. He printed ads inviting people who were looking for happiness and freedom to settle the new continent with him, and received interest from a hundred or so families. Ashinov offered to make Paissy the head of the new colony's Russian Orthodox Church and also invited Tsvetaev, who could double as a doctor and a priest.

So the adventurers boarded a ship in Odessa and set off for their promised land. Ashinov and his settlers disembarked at the French colony Obok, on the shores of the

Red Sea. They flew the Russian flag, set up camp, and named the colony New Moscow.

In response, the French government sent an inquiry to the Russian government. The latter responded that it had nothing to do with Ashinov and New Moscow. Then the French government sent a man-of-war to Obok and offered Ashinov the opportunity to remove the Russian flag and leave. He refused, probably assuming he could rely on the support of his friends in Russia. So the warship opened fire on New Moscow, killing many women and children and taking some families hostage. I no longer remember exactly what happened to Ashinov and Paissy. But Tsvetaev somehow managed to cross the impassible Danakil Desert in Africa and ended up in Abyssinia, where he befriended the Abyssinian Negus Menelik. It was this adventure that he wrote about in the *Yaroslavl Register,* if my memory serves me correctly.

❦   ❧

IN the middle of the summer of 1884, Anton took me with him to Zvenigorod. He was going there to run the local hospital while its head, Dr. Uspensky, was on vacation. He got deeply involved in the life there. Filling in for the district physician, who was also on vacation, he saw patients, performed autopsies, and gave testimony in court. The assistant pharmacist was a young man named Neapolitansky, who always managed to confuse the drugs that Anton prescribed, so Anton assigned me the task of overseeing him to make sure his patients received the correct medication.

There was a building in Zvenigorod that housed all of the government agencies, which Anton referred to in one of his stories with the line, "Here you have the police, here you have the militia, here you have the justice—a fine ladies' institution all in all." His experiences in Zvenigorod provided Anton material for "A Dead Body," "During an Autopsy," and "Siren."[12]

On one of the first days that Anton was in charge, a country boy of about five was brought in with paraphimosis. In his village such trifles usually did not get much attention, but in his case the trapping of the foreskin had caused swelling and signs of gangrene had begun to appear. The poor boy might have had to lose his manhood altogether had his parents had not brought him to the hospital in town. As Anton was about to operate, the child screamed so loudly and jerked his legs so violently that Anton was simply afraid to begin. The boy's mother was sobbing loudly, and Neapolitansky and I were hovering, curious to see the results of such an interesting operation—all of which inhibited my brother even more. Finally, he scribbled a note to Dr. P. G. Rozanov, who lived in Zvenigorod, asking him to come take a look at the boy at once. The esteemed doctor arrived promptly and performed the surgery very quickly. The boy calmed down and his mother took him back to the village. In fact, the doctor had done everything so simply and skillfully that we were almost disappointed.

Anton first met this nice doctor, if I am not mistaken, back in Voskresensk when Dr. Rozanov was visiting Dr. Arkhangelsky. But after this particular encounter they became friends and corresponded for a long time. Dr. Rozanov was a scholar; he published in medical journals and was one of the first Russian doctors to campaign for the creation of a Department of Public Health in Russia. He also dreamed of publishing a medical paper or magazine—not a narrow professional one, but one with broader appeal. But I remember that Anton talked him out of it. "The magazine will ruin you financially and age you prematurely," he said. "Besides, you will never find contributors, so you'll end up writing it all yourself." Anton was a guest at his wedding, too, and got so drunk that he remembered it for a very long time. He had been at the wedding with Dr. Uspensky and afterwards they drove "through all of Moscow," and ended up in a famous *café chantant*.[13] Anton did not make it home until the morning.

In the evenings, my brother and I would often visit L. V. Gamburtseva. She had pretty daughters and there was always music, singing, and dancing in her house. When I was a student, I liked visiting her during the Moscow winters as well. She lived on Nemetsky Street and her home was always filled with good cheer and with young folks interested in art and culture. Anton Pavlovich would stay there during his summer visits to Moscow, when the apartment was empty.

One Saturday night at her house, I met a young cadet who was not taking part in the fun. He was just sitting at the grand piano, thrumming its keys with one hand. After the dances, the hostess asked him: "Sasha, would you play something for us?" after which the young cadet immediately brightened and began playing the famous "Réminiscences des Huguenots," a very difficult composition well known now to every conservatory student and pianist.[14] The young cadet went on to become the famous virtuoso and composer A. N. Skriabin. I still regret that I did not get to know him better at the time!

L. V. Gamburtseva had two nieces, Margarita Konstantinovna and Elena Konstantinovna, known as Rita and Nelly. Rita was married to the well-known railway engineer Baron Spengler, and Nelly had just finished school. The sisters' mother had a lap dog that grumbled "nga-nga-nga," which my brother used in his story "The Teacher of Literature."[15] The Spenglers always invited young people to their house to have fun, and my brothers and I often called on them in their house on Novaya Basmannaya.

It was Anton's first year as a doctor and he still debated whether to dedicate himself to medicine or literature. The Spenglers' little children became some of Anton's first patients. In lieu of payment, the Spenglers presented him with a wallet containing a big Turkish gold coin—we called it a *lira*. That lira often helped Anton later when he fell on hard times. He would give it to me, I took it to the pawnshop, received ten rubles for it, and in a few short hours Anton's had money in his pocket again. My brother Nikolay actually courted the other sister Nelly.

The Yanovs were Anton's second patients. A. S. Yanov was an artist living in Moscow. He and my brother Nikolay had studied painting together, which was how our families met. Later, Yanov became chief designer of the Korsh Theater, and went on to work at the Leningrad Alexandrinsky Theater. During the time I am writing about, however, he was very poor and lived with his mother and three sisters—sweet young ladies. All three sisters and the mother happened to come down with typhoid at the same time. A. S. Yanov called Anton for help. Anton was a young and naive doctor willing to give up his life for someone's recovery. He spent hours and hours with those patients, exhausting himself. Despite his efforts, the women's condition worsened until one day the mother and one of the sisters died. In agony, the dying sister grabbed Anton's hand just before she passed away. Her cold handshake instilled such feelings of helplessness and guilt in Anton that he contemplated abandoning medicine altogether. And indeed, after this case he gradually switched the focus of his energies to literature and only treated the occasional patient.

The two other sisters did recover and often visited us afterwards. One of them embroidered an album with gold thread and presented it to Anton Pavlovich with the inscription "To commemorate my recovery from typhoid." Since they were both Yanovs, he nicknamed them Yashenkis. Those Yashenkis always managed to call on us when we had apple pie for dessert. As soon as apple pie appeared on the table, Anton would say: "Well, now enter the Yashenkis!" and every time the doorbell would ring.

But I have digressed. The reason why Dr. Uspensky (the doctor Anton filled in for in the Zvenigorod hospital) had come to Zvenigorod in the first place was to replace another physician, Dr. Persidsky, who had been forced to quit his job for the following reason.

Less than two miles from Zvenigorod, on the beautiful banks of the Moscow River, lay the Savinsky monastery. Its picturesque location had attracted artists like Levitan, Kuvshinnikova, Stepanov, and Aladzhalov, and it played an important role for the people of Voskresensk, too, because of the religious procession that started there. Once a year, Voskeresensk would host a celebration and a fair, and people would walk the sixteen miles from the monastery to Voskresensk.

In 1883, Yakovlev, Sirotinin, Tauber, and Sobinina, the young doctors-in-residence at Arkhangelsky's hospital, decided to take a walking trip to the Savinsky monastery. My family and a few other people joined them. We walked so briskly that we reached the monastery long before sunset, and after strolling around the monastery a bit, the young doctors decided that it would be a good idea to visit their colleague Dr. Persidsky, the head of the Zvenigorod hospital. Persidsky was delighted to see his visitors and set up an impromptu tea party in his small garden. We rested, talked, and then the young people began singing songs they had learned in school. They sang "Dubinushka," "Show Me Such an Abode," and were in the middle of another one when a police inspector suddenly arrived and began to write up a report. Persidsky tried in vain to explain that we were his guests and that choral singing was not forbidden in one's own home.

But the policeman went ahead with his report, so Persidsky decided to write a letter to the editor of the *Russian Register* to draw attention to his cause. The letter was printed but made no difference. Yakovlev had good connections in both capitals and personally went to the Moscow governor to explain what had happened, but the governor told him: "Of course, we would side with Dr. Persidsky, if he hadn't printed his letter in the *Russian Register*. But now we have to side with the Zvenigorod police so that they don't think we are scared of the *Russian Register* or that we listen to the press." And so Dr. Persidsky had to leave Zvenigorod.

AN artillery brigade was stationed about fifteen miles from Voskresensk, near Pavlovskaya. Colonel Mayevsky's battery, which was quartered in Voskresensk, was part of that brigade. One night, a brigade ball was held in Pavlovskaya. All the officers from the Voskresensk battery were expected to attend, and they took Ivan along with them. After the ball, the officers decided to spend the night in Pavlovskaya, leaving Ivan stranded (he was supposed to open the school early in the morning but, as it was winter, returning on foot was out of the question). Luckily, just as Ivan was standing on the porch, not knowing what to do, a fellow guest offered him a ride all the way back to Voskresensk in his three-horse sled.

The guest turned out to be Aleksey Kiseliov, who lived in Babkino, a village about three miles from Voskresensk. He was a nephew of the late Count Kiseliov, the Russian Ambassador to Paris. When the Count died in his palace in Nice, he left his three nephews an impressive inheritance, including some furniture that ended up at Aleksey's in Babkino. Aleksey was married to Maria Vladimirovna, the daughter of V. P. Begichev, the well-known director of the Imperial Theaters in Moscow. They had two children, a daughter named Sasha and a son named Seriozha, both of whom receive several mentions in Anton's biographies. In the course of that fateful ride back to Voskresensk he invited Ivan to be his children's private tutor, which is how the Chekhovs and the residents of Babkino established our longstanding connection. My sister Masha later befriended Maria Vladimirovna and began visiting Babkino for long periods of time, and the entire Chekhov family spent the summer of 1885 there.

As has been written many times, Babkino played an important role in the development of Anton's talent. I will not dwell on the enchanting natural beauty of this place where we could freely enjoy the large English park, the river, the woods, and the meadows. The people in Babkino felt perfectly matched for our family. The Kiseliovs were one of those rare families who knew how to marry tradition with modern culture. Kiseliov's father-in-law, Begichev (portrayed as Ashanin in Boleslav Markevich's novel *A Quarter Century Ago*), was an utterly fascinating individual. He was receptive to art and literature, and we would sit in his room, with its feminine furnishings, listening to the stories of his adventures in Russia and abroad for hours. Anton owes the stories "The Death of a Government Official" (an incident that really happened at the Bolshoy Theater in Moscow) and "Volodia" to him. "The Burbot" was also based on a real event that happened during the construction of a pool in Babkino, while "The Daughter of Albion" was inspired by our time there—the milieu and characters are all from there.[16] Meanwhile in the park, as Anton put it, "roamed the ghost of Boleslav Markevich," who only a year earlier lived in Babkino and wrote his *Abyss* there.[17]

Babkino was full of interesting people. Maria Vladimirovna was the granddaughter of the well-known publisher and humanist writer Novikov, and she too wrote for magazines. She was also a passionate fisherman and would stand for hours on the riverbank, holding her rod and discussing literature with Anton and Masha. Vladislavlev, a celebrated tenor, also lived there, and would sing his songs and arias for us. He had been famous for the song "On the Mountain over the River is a Village," and could still hold the high D note in the word "Hey!" for a whole minute. Maria Vladimirovna sang, too. E. A. Efremova played us Beethoven, Liszt, and other great composers. The Kiseliovs were close friends with Dargomyzhsky, Piotr Tchaikovsky, and Salvini[18] so the conversation was often about music, composers, and the art of drama. Tchaikovsky had just premiered *Eugene Onegin* and was on everyone's mind. Meanwhile, the beautiful children ran around the English park, trading jokes with Anton and making life altogether merrier. People like the hunter Ivan Gavrilov, an uncanny liar (like all hunters); the gardener Vassily Ivanovich, who divided all vegetation into *trapika* and *botanika;* the carpenters, who were building the bathing hut; peasants; sick women, who came to be treated; and, finally, nature herself— all gave my brother Anton ideas for stories and plots and had a very positive impact on him.

Everybody in Babkino woke up very early. Anton was already at his desk writing by about seven in the morning. The desk was actually a converted sewing machine placed in front of a big square window, which offered Anton a magnificent view whenever he looked up from his writing. During this time, he contributed to *Fragments* and *The Saint Petersburg Gazette* and generously shared his impressions of Babkino. Lunch was early, too, at about one in the afternoon. Anton loved picking mushrooms and claimed it was easier for him to think up new ideas for his stories in the woods. The lonely Polevshchin Church stood near the Daraganov forest and always fascinated Anton. Services were held only once a year there, during the Kazanskaya,[19] and at night the sexton rang the church bell every hour on the hour and its doleful toll reached all the way to Babkino. The church and its tiny sexton's house by the mail road inspired Anton's stories "The Witch" and "Evil Deed."[20]

After Anton's walk in the woods, we would have tea, and then Anton would sit down to write again. In the evenings, we played croquet and dined at eight o'clock.

After dinner, we would all go over to the Kiseliovs' big house. Those were magical, unforgettable evenings. In the course of those nights, we would talk a great deal about literature and the arts, relishing the works of Turgenev and Pisemsky.[21] We were voracious readers; everybody subscribed to all the literary magazines and many newspapers. Later on, Kiseliov and Begichev would play solitaire, while E. A. Efremova played the piano and Vladislavlev sang. The whole Chekhov family would gather around Maria Vladimirovna and listen to her stories about Tchaikovsky, Dargomyzhsky, Rossi, and Salvini. I can state unequivocally that Anton's love of music developed right then and there. Maria Vladimirovna made no secret of the fact that she liked Tchaikovsky a lot and that he had once been in love with her. In the days when she was still single, he had wanted to propose to her but was simply too late. Here is how Maria Vladimirovna told the story.

As I said before, Maria's father, Begichev, was director of what was then called the Imperial Theaters. After his wife died, he married M. V. Shilovskaya, a famous singer, and Maria Vladimirovna, then a beautiful woman of twenty, suddenly became her stepdaughter. She was forced to live under the same roof with her Father and his new wife, who, it turned out, was very jealous of her.

The Begichevs always kept their doors open and their large apartment was a meeting place for all of Moscow. Tchaikovsky and other celebrities from the music and theater world were frequent visitors. Everyone was young, fresh, and interesting, and it was only natural that they should cluster around the house's younger mistress. Shilovskaya was older and already had adult sons (one of whom, K. S. Shilovsky, was the author of the once-famous love song "Little Tiger"—the song with the line, "In the night sky floats the moon . . ."). Jealous of the attention her stepdaughter received, Shilovskaya made Maria's life miserable. The dynamic was so obvious that the young men in Maria's circle could not help but notice it. One day at dinner, Maria was so offended by her stepmother that she burst out sobbing. She left the table and ran into the other room. Kiseliov, who was one of the guests at the table, followed after her and found himself spontaneously proposing to her. "Things couldn't be any worse," she replied, accepting his proposal. Tchaikovsky arrived just after Kiseliov, and offered his own proposal, but by then it was too late. "And happiness was so possible, so close . . ."[22]

Thanks to this episode and to his opera *Eugene Onegin,* the marvelous Tchaikovsky always held a special fascination for me. Providence allowed me the good fortune of meeting him in our home in mid-October of 1889. He was down-to-earth and without pretension, and after sitting with us for a while, he drew from his pocket a photograph with the inscription, "To A. P. Chekhov, from his passionate admirer. October 14, 1889. P. Tchaikovsky," and handed it to Anton.

Their conversation touched on music and literature, and in particular I remember them discussing the content of the libretto for the opera *Bela,* which Tchaikovsky was planning to compose. Tchaikovsky wanted Anton to write a libretto based on Lermontov's story.[23] Bela would be the soprano, Pechorin the baritone, Maxim Maximych the tenor, and Kazbich would be the bass. "Only—you know what, Anton Pavlovich?" said Tchaikovsky. "I wouldn't want marching processions. To be honest, I don't like marches." That visit and his charming personality made a deep impression on all of us. Anton thanked Tchaikovsky for the photograph by dedicating his next book, *Gloomy People,*[24] to him.

Anton's previous book, *In the Twilight,* had been dedicated to the writer D. V. Grigorovich.[25] This is how it happened:

When we lived on Kudrinskaya-Sadovaya in the Korneev house, Anton published a short story called "The Gamekeeper"[26] in *The Saint Petersburg Gazette.* Soon after, Anton received a letter from Grigorovich: "You have got a real talent, a talent that puts you way above this new generation of writers. . . . As you can see, I couldn't resist, and am reaching out to you with all my heart." The old writer was the first to recognize the breadth of Anton's talent and to bestow his blessings on him. Of course, this letter overwhelmed Anton and the rest of us, both with its unexpectedness and the extent of its praise. Anton immediately sat down and wrote his famous response to Grigorovich (the letter is the one with the line, "My dear and much-loved bearer of good tidings, your letter struck me like a bolt of lightning," from March 26, 1886). Then Grigorovich sent him his portrait with the inscription, "From an old writer to a young talent," all of which led to the old writer and the young talent developing a friendship. Anton took a trip to Saint Petersburg, visited Grigorovich there, and came back intoxicated by his warm reception. Aleksey Suvorin even invited Anton to write for his newspaper as a result. From this point on, money was no longer so tight, and our circumstances began to improve.

I was now an enthusiastic university student; Masha had developed into a charming, kind, and educated young woman; and Anton was twenty-five. Our apartment became a haven filled with young people, interesting young women with a penchant for arts, music, and literature—including Lika Mizinova,[27] Dasha Musin-Pushkina, and Varia Eberle—filled our second-story living room with music, song, and dance. Anton drew inspiration from all the sounds and people and spent a lot of time at work in his study downstairs. He would sometimes take a break to come upstairs and joke or horse around with the rest of us. During the day when everybody was otherwise occupied and there were no visitors, he would often say to me, "Misha, play something, would you? I can't write like this." I did play for him—sometimes for a half an hour straight. I'd play songs from popular musicals and did it with as much frenetic zeal as a sanguine second-year university student could muster.

Our friends came by nightly, but one evening, quite unexpectedly, Grigorovich himself showed up. Tall, slender, handsome, and casually decked out in an expensive tie, he made himself right at home and immediately began flirting with the young ladies! He spent the entire evening with us, staying well into the wee hours. Dasha Musin-Pushkina enchanted him so much that he escorted her all the way to her apartment door.

The second time Grigorovich and I met we were at the Suvorins' in Saint Petersburg. He began recounting the night he had spent in our house and clearly remembered it fondly. "Anna Ivanovna, my dear," he said to Suvorin's wife excitedly, "If you only knew what was going on at the Chekhovs'!" Raising both arms to the sky he exclaimed: "Bacchanalia, my sweetheart, true bacchanalia!"

Let me get back to Babkino. All of us, including Anton, were happy there, thanks in large part to its residents' liveliness and good nature. He wrote and all of the critics except for A. Skabichevsky praised his work. He predicted that Anton would become an alcoholic and die in a ditch, but Anton was confident enough that it did not bother him. Also, at the time, he was still in good health.

From time to time Anton would put aside his work and act silly. One summer night, he and his artist friend I. Levitan[28] put on Oriental robes. Anton covered his face with soot, donned a turban, and, toting a rifle, went into the field across the river, accompanied by Levitan on the back of a donkey. Dismounting, Levitan placed a rug on the ground and, facing east like a real Muslim, started to pray. Suddenly the "Bedouin," Anton, crept up from behind the bushes with a rifle. He shot a blank and Levitan fell flat on his back. They called this "playing the Orient," and they would do it to entertain us.

Another entertainment was to conduct a fake court hearing, with Levitan as the defendant, Kiseliov the judge, and Anton the prosecutor. Anton would put on special makeup and they would both wear the old gilded uniforms from Kiseliov and Begichev's closets. Anton's closing argument always made us roar with laughter. Sometimes, Anton would pretend to be a dentist and make me dress up as a servant girl. His "visiting patients" would trouble me for such extra niceties that I would lose my composure and burst out laughing instead.

In Babkino we occupied the same wing as the writer Boleslav Markevich had when he lived there. I met him, his wife, and their son when I visited the Kiseliovs in the summer of 1884. Markevich resembled the marble statue of the Commendatore, owing to his white hair, white whiskers, and his propensity for dressing head to toe in white. Even though I liked his novel,[29] I can't say I felt the same way about Markevich. Many people speculated about why he had been summarily dismissed from his job, and he was said to be an enemy of Turgenev. I adored Turgenev and read his highly critical response to one of Markevich's arguments in the *European Herald*. I also knew that Markevich held views similar to those of the conservative *Moscow Bulletin*.[30] But I still admired him as a writer, especially his prose style.

Markevich was very bored in Babkino. He missed the hubbub of the city, and especially daily access to newspapers and magazines. To get his hands on them before anyone else, Markevich would walk all the way to the woods to meet Mikeshka the servant on his way back from the post office. He would take all of the newspapers from him, and not share them with anyone else until he had perused each one from cover to cover.

One afternoon in late August, when the gloom of autumn is beginning in Northern Russia and the vacationing urbanites are contemplating their return to city life, Markevich set out on his usual trip to the woods. He intercepted Mikeshka and seized the newspapers from him. For once he didn't need to hide, because the others were all outside playing croquet, and so he sat himself down in the Kiseliovs' big house. All dressed in white, as always, he parked himself at the dining table under the oil lamp and began to read. He put on his golden pince-nez, turned his back to the lamp, and dove into the papers. After a while he felt the light dimming, so without looking at the lamp, he turned up the knob. He did this a few times as it grew dark outside. By the time we got back to the house after croquet, the lamp was smoking like a volcano. The room was filled with floating clouds of soot, the tablecloth was entirely singed, and so was Markevich himself—his venerable white mane and his impeccable suit had both gone completely black.

Amazingly, Babkino also played a prominent role in the artistic development of Levitan, the founder of the Russian landscape school. Our family had known him from the days when he and Nikolay studied together at the College of

Painting, Sculpture, and Architecture in Moscow. They were close friends and helped each other in their work. For example, one of Levitan's paintings in the Tretiakov Gallery depicts a lady walking down an alley in Sokolniky in the fall. Nikolay actually painted the lady, while Levitan returned the favor by painting the sky in Nikolay's *Messalina*.

When we first went to spend the summer in Babkino, Levitan happened to be staying in the nearby village of Maximovka, which was about three miles from us, across the river on the big Klinsky road. Whenever he went there to paint, Levitan rented a place from Vassily, an alcoholic potter who lived in the village with his perpetually pregnant wife Pelageya.

As was well known, Levitan occasionally suffered from depression. During these bouts, he would either take his shotgun and leave home for a week or two or sit at home, silent and sullen and all alone. He would mope around the house with his arms crossed on his chest and his head lowered until he felt better.

One week, we had several days in a row of rain. It was monotonous, depressing, and endless. The potter's wife came to complain about her ailments and mentioned that her renter, Tessak Ilyich (she was referring to Isaak Ilyich Levitan), had fallen sick. We were pleasantly surprised to learn that Levitan was so close to Babkino, and Anton wanted to see him. Because of the rain, we did not go to the Kiseliovs' that evening, and the night ahead promised to be long and boring. After supper, Anton proposed, "You know what? Let's go see Levitan now!"

Anton, Ivan, and I put on tall boots, took a lamp, and walked into the darkness. We crossed the river, jumping from stone to stone, then splashed through a few soggy meadows and a swamp, and finally entered the thick and dark Daraganov forest. Our feeble lamp could barely light our way. The centuries-old firs and bushes grabbed at us in the dark and we could feel thick torrents of water pouring through the branches. Finally, we reached Maximovka. We were able to figure out which house was the potter's by the clay shards strewn around the yard. Without knocking or announcing ourselves, we broke into Levitan's room, and shone the light right into his eyes. Jumping from the bed, Levitan aimed his revolver at us until, squinting in the light, he finally recognized us and exclaimed, "Darn it! What fools! R-r-r-really stupid fools!" We all sat around laughing at Anton's prank, and our visit definitely raised Levitan's spirits.

A little while later Levitan moved to Babkino to be closer to us. Anton insisted that I move in with him, so I wound up under the same roof as Levitan. One of the Chekhovs wrote a verse that went like this:

Here is the wing of Levitan,
An artist sweet like marzipan.
An early morning's devotee
He's up at dawn and drinks his tea.

Levitan had a wonderfully noble face. I have rarely seen such expressive eyes or such an artistic combination of lines and features. He had a long nose but it somehow suited the rest of his face perfectly. The artist Polenov used Levitan's face for his portrayal of Christ in his famous painting *Christ and the Adulteress*. Women found him very attractive. He knew it, too, and was a terrible flirt. His affairs went on publicly and were always tumultuous and turbulent. They had all the stupid things characteristic of love affairs, including a few gunshots, even. If he found a woman who interested him, he would drop everything to pursue her, sometimes quite literally giving chase, even outside Moscow. He would think nothing of kneeling in front of a woman no matter where he happened to be at the moment, whether in a public park or at someone's house. Some women liked that about him, but some were afraid to be compromised and avoided him, even though they were secretly drawn to him. Once he was challenged to a duel at the symphony hall in the middle of a concert. During the intermission, he asked me to be his second.

Another of his love affairs came close to ruining his friendship with Anton.

Dimitry Pavlovich Kuvshinnikov, a physician in the police department, was married to Sofia Petrovna and lived in a state-owned apartment under the watchtower of a Moscow fire station. Sofia took painting lessons from Levitan so he and another artist named Stepanov visited the Kuvshinnikovs frequently. Dimitry Pavlovich worked day and night and Sofia painted while he was away.[31] Some of her paintings are now in the Tretiakov Gallery. She was not a very attractive woman, but her talent made her interesting.

She dressed very well and could create an elegant outfit out of almost anything. She brought the same rare gift to decorating; even a barn would feel comfortable and cozy after she was finished with it. In their apartment, everything seemed luxurious and stylish, even though their "Turkish sofas" were really just boxes covered with mattresses wrapped in carpet and their curtains were simple fishing nets.

Their house always attracted many visitors: doctors, artists, musicians, and writers. I always really liked going there and enjoyed the evenings of loud conversations, music, and singing. But we never saw the master of the house among the guests. Around midnight, the dining room doors would open to reveal the doctor's large frame holding a fork in one hand and a knife in another, and he would solemnly announce: "Ladies and gentlemen, kindly proceed to eat."

At the request, everybody would tumble into the dining room. The table would be literally covered with an abundance of hors d'oeuvres. Then Sofia Petrovna would run up to her husband, delighted, and grab his face with her both hands exclaiming: "Dimitry Kuvshinnikov!" (She would often use his last name.) "Ladies and gentlemen, please look at this expressive and wonderful face of his!"

In the summer, artists usually left Moscow to paint on the Volga River or near Zvenigorod, in the village of Savinskaya. They would live together in communes for months at a time. So Levitan left for the Volga to paint and live in one of the communes, and Sofia Petrovna went too and stayed for the entire summer. Levitan went to Savinskaya the following year, again with Sofia Petrovna as his student. People around them started to talk but Sofia Petrovna seemed as tender and sincere to her husband as before. She would still grab his head with both hands, and adoringly exclaim: "Dimitry Kuvshinnikov! Let me shake your honest hand! Ladies and gentlemen, look at this noble face!"

After a lot of wine, Dr. Kuvshinnikov finally poured out his heart to Stepanov. Apparently, he did suspect what was going on, but preferred to suffer in silence.

Anton was critical of Sofia Petrovna and unable to conceal his feelings; he wrote a story called "The Butterfly," based on the situation.[32] However, Dymov's death in the story was made up.

When this story was printed in *North,* some of our friends criticized Anton for disguising the identity of his characters too thinly, while others simply giggled and gloated. Levitan sulked. Anton dismissed the matter with jokes like, "My butterfly is pretty at least, but Sofia Petrovna is neither beautiful nor young." The rumor was that Levitan was going to challenge Anton to a duel. The quarrel lasted for a long time. I do not know how it would have ended if T. L. Shchepkina-Kupernik[33] had not practically dragged Levitan to Anton for a reconciliation.

Sofia Petrovna died, her husband died; but Levitan still continued his affairs. One of them, incidentally, is connected to *The Seagull.* I do not know all the details of how my brother came up with *The Seagull*'s plot, but here is what I do know. One summer, Levitan was living on a big estate somewhere up north by the railroad and got involved in a very complicated affair there, which ended very badly. To get himself out of it, he decided he needed to kill himself or, at the very least, make it look like he had tried to kill himself. He shot himself in the head, and although the bullet only grazed his skull, the female players in this drama were still very alarmed. They knew that Anton was a physician and that he was friends with Levitan, so they sent him an urgent telegram to come help. Reluctantly, Anton went. When he came back, he told me that Levitan had covered his head wound with a black bandage, which he threw on the floor during his conversation with the two women. One of the nights Anton was there, Levitan went to the lake with a shotgun. When he returned to one of his lovers, he was carrying a dead seagull which he had shot for no reason, and he threw it at her feet. These are the two details that Anton used in *The Seagull.* Sofia Petrovna Kuvshinnikova tried to claim that she was the heroine of that scene. This is not true, at least not according to what my late brother told me. I will of course admit the possibility that Levitan repeated the same scene more than once.

VI

THE FIRST
PLAYS

I FOUND OUT THAT I HAD BEEN ADMITTED TO MOSCOW University the first summer that we vacationed in Babkino. The university had just enacted a new charter that called for mandatory uniforms, on-campus detention cells, and other "niceties" associated with the Pobedonostsev[1] regime. The professors were obligated to instill patriotic ideas in the students. Among the ideas they were expected to instill was the belief that Russia was the country *sui generis,* that His Imperial Majesty was the only rightful source of power in the state, that a constitution and its related institutions would be bad for the country, that the West had lost its way, and finally that self-governance just did not agree with the spirit and character of the Russian people.

Such "transgressions" as students applauding their professors were seen as the pinnacle of free-thinking. Guilty students were randomly snatched from the classroom and sent to detention cells. I was even sent there once, because I was mistakenly thought to have been at a lecture where students applauded Professor Kovalevsky. One petty administrator, Pavlov, became a real tyrant; he was so quick to punish for the smallest trespass that in his presense students were literally on their tiptoes. Not surprisingly, when the university was shut down for six months, Pavlov easily found other suitable employment: he became a regular policeman and was stationed right there, across the street from the campus.

Many university faculty members were puppets of the state. Once, when the tsar's family visited the university, I saw a trustee of the Moscow educational district, P. A. Kapnist, kiss the tsar's hand so passionately and with such wet lips that the tsar pulled his hand back in disgust. The trustee was in such a state of sycophantic rapture that he still kept trying to catch the tsar's hand in the air and kiss it.

The new charter prohibited students from printing lectures because the university was afraid that students might print political proclamations instead. This repressive atmosphere made it difficult for us students to study. The professors continued to deliver their usual courses, completely disregarding the material Pobedonostsev required us to be tested on. This meant that we never understood what was required of us, and took the university tests purely perfunctorily.

After we had muddled our way through the entire course, we had to take the state examination. The exam results were deplorable because we were expected to know the Department of Education material, even though it had not been taught to us. It was as if we had taken two courses: one through the lectures of our professors and another through textbooks written by strangers. Of the 346 students who took the exam, only 49 received a diploma.

Perhaps it was no accident that the chair of the examination committee was the prosecutor for the Moscow Judicial District, N. V. Muraviov—who also happened to be the prosecuting attorney during the March 1 trial.[2] But in this case, he took the students' side right from the beginning, and during the exams sent telegrams to Secretary Delianov requesting waivers of the official policy. Unexpectedly, the Department of Education cooperated. This meant that neither the chair nor any members of the committee were in the room during the final exams and that the exams were given by the individual professors, who could finally follow their own program. Before the exam on ecclesiastical law, a difficult and voluminous subject, we asked Professor A. S. Pavlov not to be overly strict with us. "Overly strict?" said the old man. "The order has been to have you all pass!" And he gave us all "satisfactory" grades, without even testing us.

My brother Anton had been a doctor for a whole year by the time I was accepted to university. We lived in Yakimanka then, and his apartment door had a plaque that read "Doctor A. P. Chekhov," even though he still hadn't decided whether to stick with literature or be a full-time physician. It was boring to live so far away from the city center and its theaters, so Anton designated Tuesdays as open-house days to retain some semblance of a social life. He did not have much money, so the main attraction for the guests was our Mother's special jellied pikeperch.

On the corner of Bolshaya Nikitskaya and Brusovsky Alley, across the street from the conservatory, stood a very old building. Furnished rooms nicknamed "Bear Rooms" occupied the first floor, and they were taken by the poorest people, mostly conservatory pupils and other students. It was a close-knit, friendly community. When one of them had a visitor, everyone contributed whatever money they had, regardless of whether or not they knew the visitor. Even the bellboy was bohemian. He always managed to buy a lot of food with the forty kopecks he collected from everyone. He stuttered, so talking to him was both entertaining and challenging. "So, what did you buy, Piotr?" "Errr-r-r-r-r, he-he-herring and t-t-t-t-wo cu-cu-cu-cu-cu-uuucumbers and a half bottle of vo-vo-vo-vo-vo-dka."

Our brother Nikolay moved into one of the rooms and quickly became friends with the other tenants. He brought some of his new friends from the Bear Rooms with him to our Tuesday night open house, including B. M. Azanchevsky (who later became a well-known composer and conductor), V. S. Tyutynik (who became a bass in the Bolshoy Opera), M. R. Semashko (a cellist in the same opera), the pianist N. V. Dolgov, and the flutist A. I. Ivanenko. From the beginning, Anton's evening receptions in Yakimanka had a distinctly musical flavor.

As the years passed, "the stormy wind scattered remnants of former dreams,"[3] and the friends who came to the Yakimanka receptions settled down, became family men, and disappeared from our circles. Only the flutist Ivanenko remained close to our family, even after Anton moved to Yalta. I think Anton drew certain traits of Yepikhodov in *The Cherry Orchard*[4] from Ivanenko.

In March of 1888, after we moved from Yakimanka to Kudrinskaya-Sadovaya, our family started discussing where we should go for the summer. The spring came early and the pull of the countryside's green pastures was strong. We did not want to go to Babkino again, because Anton needed new places and new creative ideas. He developed a suspicious-sounding cough and had been talking about the south, perhaps renting a summer house in either Sviatye Gory in the Kharkov province or in Karantin, near Taganrog. Ivanenko was Ukrainian, from the town of Sumy in Kharkov, and when he heard that Anton was thinking of heading south, he grabbed him, made a passionate speech about his homeland, and advised us to vacation there and only there. He mentioned the Lintvariov family, who lived in Luka near Sumy and had a place to rent. Anton wrote to them and received a positive response, but he could not bring himself to rent the summer place sight unseen—he thought it was too risky to take such a long trip with the entire family without more information about the place and its owners.

I was a third-year student at the time. I had earned
eighty-two rubles from copying lectures and publishing children's stories, and was planning to take a trip to Taganrog
and Crimea until the money ran out, and then return to the
north. I did not approve of the decision to go to Ukraine for
the summer; I had grown used to Babkino and felt a great
affinity for its residents. But my brother had something else
in mind. Just as I was about to leave Moscow on April 17, he
made a request. Anton asked me not to go directly to the
south, but to head to Sumy instead. He wanted me to visit
the Lintvariovs, look at the summer house in Luka, and send
him my impressions. This excursion was not part of my plans
at all, but nevertheless, I went.

After well-kept Babkino, Luka made a dismal impression on me. The estate felt neglected. There was a permanent puddle in the middle of the courtyard, which boasted
huge, wallowing swine and a collection of ducks gliding on
its surface. The park looked like a primeval forest—not
only was it wild and overgrown, it had actual graves in it.
The liberal Lintvariovs saw me wearing my student uniform and immediately assumed that I was a reactionary. All
in all, my initial impression of Luka was far from favorable.
I wrote Anton from the road, advising him not to rush into
the move to Sumy.

But while I was roaming around Taganrog and Crimea,
Anton rented the Luka house anyway, and moved there
with our Mother and sister in the first week of May. By the
time I had returned from my southern journey, they were
settled in and Anton was already hosting the poet Aleksey
Nikolaevich Pleshcheev.[5] The old man had come from

Saint Petersburg, which was a great feat considering his advanced age. Everybody in Luka venerated him as if he were a miracle-working icon.

The Lintvariov family consisted of a kind old mother and five adult children. Two daughters were doctors, one was a university graduate, one son was an accomplished pianist, and the other was a political dropout from the university. All of them were wonderfully kind people, affectionate and caring but—I would venture to say—not all that happy. Having visitors like Anton and Pleshcheev, whose poetry they adored, pleased them immensely.

When Aleksey Nikolaevich came calling, they would place him on an old sofa and gather around him, listening spellbound to his stories. Have no doubt, there was a lot to hear. He had a good heart and being surrounded by young people seemed to breathe new life into him; his face would flush, his eyes would sparkle with joy, and he would gesticulate wildly. When he recited his famous poem "Forward, my friends, without fear, to feats of prowess and glory,"—even the most inveterate skeptic could not help but think that "the dawn of sacred redemption" might actually be in the sky.

The story of Pleshcheev's involvement in the Petrashevsky Affair[6] always made a huge impression on his listeners. In 1849, he was captured, thrown into Peter and Paul Fortress, tried, and sentenced to death by hanging. And so, the day came when he was placed in the formidable chariot and taken to Semionovsky Platz. He was led to the scaffold, and a cerement was put on him. The executioner had already fitted the noose over his neck when the officer supervising the execution suddenly whispered, "You've been pardoned!" A courier galloped in and announced that Tsar Nikolay I, in his "infinite" mercy, had "deigned" to change the death sentence to exile in Turkestan and demotion to a rank-and-file soldier. Pleshcheev spent seven years in exile, fought at Ak-Mechet, received amnesty from Alexander II, and finally came back home to Saint Petersburg. In spite of all the suffering he had endured, Pleshcheev was always exuberant and vigorous. Despite being a wonderful poet, he was poor his whole life and had had to do editorial work and even secretly translate to make ends meet. During his visit to Luka, he wrote poems. He was given his own room, which the young ladies always decorated with fresh flowers. There, early in the morning, he would sit at his desk and write poetry, reciting each line aloud. Sometimes it sounded like he was calling for help, so someone would run to his room to assist and wind up startling him.

Pleshcheev loved anything made with flour. To please him, our Mother fed him dumplings, pies, and other home-made delicacies. Often after such feasts, he would lie down on his back and moan because he was so full. Anton would bring him a hot-water bottle and forbid him from overindulging in food. The old man always forgot about his discomfort in time for the next feast.

After a lifetime of being poor, Pleshcheev suddenly became very rich: About a year and a half before his death, he inherited a million rubles. He went to Paris and people saw him there wearing a top hat, dressed like a dandy. In a cruel twist of fate, however, another heir turned up. The money was taken from the old poet, and he was destitute for the rest of his days. He died in Paris soon afterwards, in 1893. His body was transported to Moscow and interred at the Novodevichy monastery, not far from where Anton's grave would later be.

Our family's close relationship with the Lintvariovs outlasted that summer in Luka by many years. Just like in Babkino, there was a lot of music and conversation about literature; especially when M. R. Semashko, the cellist I wrote about before, came to visit. Sometimes, we went fishing and crayfish hunting. Other times we got into boats and paddled to the mill or to the birch woods on the other side of the river and cooked porridge there.

Anton wrote a lot, but life in Ukraine did not inspire him as much as Babkino had; it seemed to leave him cold. A teacher named Lidia Fiodorovna was responsible for such pearls as "a linden alley lined with Lombardy poplars." But I think that was the extent of it. Anton's writing in Luka tended to explore themes that he brought from home. If he observed life around him, it was only ethnographically.

No sooner had Pleshcheev left Luka than another writer, Kazimir Stanislavovich Barantsevich, arrived. He was a very humble man, not too old but already bald. He had worked hard all his life but still lived in near poverty. From what I heard, he had begun his life of drudgery as a brick seller in a shop. Once he began writing and publishing, his career blossomed quickly; literary critics took note and dubbed them a trio—"Chekhov, Barantsevich, and Korolenko." But the financial demands of his large family and his work in the Horse-Drawn and Railway Transportation Association in Saint Petersburg proved too great a distraction from literature, and he gradually abandoned it. The poor man had to get up at four o'clock in the morning in order to get to his desk by five and start issuing tickets to the conductors. Later, he attempted to publish a children's magazine that I believe was called *Red Dawns*. But the magazine didn't stand out and was ultimately unsuccessful.

And now Barantsevich, who had never traveled any farther beyond Saint Petersburg than Pargolovo or Ozerky, had gathered his courage, rallied his spirits, and taken a trip all the way to Ukraine to visit us. One can imagine the joy he felt at being in our company.

He seemed like a genuinely decent person and an enjoyable conversationalist, although he could also be a bit sentimental. When it came time to return to his home and his transport office, he did it unwillingly. We remembered him fondly for a long time after he left. He had accidentally left behind a pair of pants and, as they say "to forget something is to return for it," we hoped he would return to Luka. But he did not.

After Barantsevich, Suvorin, the publisher of *New Time*,[7] and the actor P. M. Svobodin[8] came to visit. Anton's friendship with these two men had begun during the production of his play *Ivanov* at the Alexandrinsky Theater in Saint Petersburg. Although he had known Suvorin before through his work for *New Time*, the visit to Luka served to strengthen their friendship. Anton had a very high opinion of Suvorin, even though he did not share the views expressed in *New Time.* But he was able to separate the man from the newspaper and valued his friendship a great deal. For several years, he wrote very frank letters to him, expressing his most intimate thoughts and feelings.

About a mile from the estate where we lived was a big sixteen-wheel roller mill. Surrounded by old oak woods, it occupied an idyllic location on the Psiol River. Anton and Suvorin would often go fishing near the mill in a simple dugout canoe made out of a tree trunk. They would stand by the mill's wheels for hours, fishing rods in hand, talking about literature and society.

It was actually through Suvorin that I met the esteemed Anatoly Fiodorovich Koni.[9] I had seen many of his father's vaudevilles and respected his scholarly and literary writings, but I had never met him. One day, Suvorin asked me to deliver a packet to A. F. Koni's office. He was alone when I got there, and I decided to introduce myself. Koni was a member of the Academy of Science and we discussed the Pushkin Award that the academy had recently awarded Anton. I was just about to leave when Koni shifted the conversation from the Pushkin Award to Pushkin himself. I was amazed by the fact that he knew all of Pushkin's work by heart. He recited his poems with ardor and even raised his arms in the air as if performing Pushkin on stage. When the conversation returned to the subject of my brother, Koni became emotional and his voice trembled. His mostly shaved face, with a little beard like that of an English Quaker, wore a very tender, almost paternal expression: "Ah, what a talent he is! What an important and wonderful talent he is!"

Later, after my own literary career had been launched, Koni delivered a talk at the Academy of Science on my book *Essays and Stories,* which went on to receive an honorable mention. That was a great surprise for me.

Suvorin lived an interesting life. Unlike his father, a common soldier who had fought at Borodino, Suvorin became a parish teacher and taught in district colleges in Bobrov and Voronezh. His passion for literature drew him to start writing, a little verse here and prose trifles there, and to publish in various metropolitan magazines. Finally, after he was made a permanent contributor to Countess Salias's *Russian Language* in the early 1860s, he moved to Moscow.

He would often tell me about that period of his life, which he took great pleasure in recalling. He had a habit of pacing back and forth, and I remember feeling tired just watching him move, but I always listened intently. He narrated his stories with imagery and humor, with a wonderful use of similes, and would digress as new thoughts popped into his mind.

He told me that he had arrived in Moscow with the hope of finding a literary job that paid enough to live on. When one did not materialize, he found himself living in abject poverty. Too poor even to live in Moscow proper, he instead settled in Mazilovo, a small village about four and a half miles from the city. Every day, he would walk from the village to the city—barefoot, in order to save his boots. When his wife was pregnant and close to delivering, he did not have a spare kopeck for a midwife and grew really desperate. One day, despondent and helpless, he sat down on a bench on Sretensky Boulevard. Anton told me this next part of the story. While he was sitting there, a young man carrying a big portfolio sat next to him. They started talking and the young man was touched by Suvorin's situation. He reached into his pocket and pulled out a packet with five wax seals. "Here, my dear mother sent me fifteen rubles. I just collected them from the post office. Please take them if you want."

It was a godsend to Suvorin. He asked the young man who he was so he could someday repay the debt. The man turned out to be V. P. Burenin, then a student at the College of Painting, Sculpture, and Architecture but who later gained fame as a pamphleteer and critic at *New Time*.[10]

From Moscow, Suvorin moved to Saint Petersburg and became an associate at the *Saint Petersburg Register*.[11] He wrote under the names "A. Bobrovsky" and "Neznakomets." It was his heyday as a journalist. His critical essays were read by everyone and he was always spot-on in his criticisms of the bigwigs of the day. He did it so skillfully that it was hard to find fault, but he was still once sentenced to six months in jail.

Because the *Saint Petersburg Register* was a government-sponsored paper, Suvorin's satirical articles eventually led to the paper being taken away from V. F. Korsh and, after a bribe, leased to a new publisher. Naturally, during the transition, "Neznakomets" was removed from the staff. Suvorin then moved to the *Exchange Register* and continued his Sunday articles there.

He worked there until 1876, when the Herzegovina unrest spread in the Balkan Peninsula and pulled Russia into the Russian-Turkish War. At that time, Suvorin was able to acquire the newspaper *New Time* at a bargain price. He delegated the day-to-day duties to his wife and went off to war as a reporter. He managed to establish connections within Prince Milan of Serbia's staff and got insider information about even the smallest skirmishes, which allowed his newspaper to break the story first. His wife would then send the hot-off-the-presses papers to the front, where they sold out within minutes to the officers of the Russian army. Only in *New Time* could they learn the details of the battles they had just fought and find out who had won. The war coverage led to the paper's great success. The paper's main subscribers continued to be military and civilian officials, which is how the paper acquired its specific character.

As Suvorin aged, his children by his first wife began to take over the paper. He withdrew from it almost entirely and continued to publish only his passionate "Little Letters," which still hinted at his former alter ego Neznakomets. He immersed himself in studies of the Time of Troubles, the history of literature, and dramaturgy. It was around this time that he and Anton got to know one another. Suvorin also loved books passionately and had a hand in changing the publishing industry by drastically decreasing the price of a book. For example, he published a ten-volume set of Pushkin's works and sold it for only one and a half rubles.

Unfortunately, it was also around this time that his newspaper increased its intolerance toward national minorities. Even people who were generally indifferent to the question were appalled by the paper's inexplicably frantic zeal against Finland, Poland, and the Baltic provinces, not to mention the Jews. This intolerance reached its peak in 1898, during the notorious Dreyfus Affair in Paris, which captured the imagination of many Europeans and Americans.

Both Anton and Suvorin came from the lower classes, were the grandchildren of former serfs, were naturally gifted beyond measure and well-educated, and both felt great affection for each other. But when *New Time* unfairly took the side of Dreyfus's accusers, it strained their friendship.[12] The old man loved Anton until his death, but Anton distanced himself from Suvorin while the Dreyfus case was still under investigation. He wrote to Suvorin less and less frequently—the separation of time and distance helped—until finally the correspondence, which had contained so many wonderful thoughts, so many new and original insights, and had revealed so much of Anton's inner landscape, ended.

THE actor Pavel Matveevich Svobodin visited us at our summer retreat in Luka a few times. He had acted in both of the Saint Petersburg productions of Anton's *Ivanov* and Suvorin's *Tatiana Repina* in 1889, in the course of which he and Anton had become friends. Pavel Matveevich—or as we called him jokingly in French, "Paul-Matias"—and my brother Anton were both outstanding comedians, their inexhaustible array of jokes and witty pranks made everybody in Luka laugh.

For example, they once went fishing with Pavel decked out in tails and top hat. Just imagine a man standing on a reedy riverbank wearing a white shirt and tie, tails, a top hat, and white gloves, holding his fishing rod with the most serious face imaginable as peasants passed by in their dugouts. Another time, we all went on a trip to Akhtyrka, a backwater town, where we stayed in a local inn. Pavel pretended to be a count and Anton his servant, an arrangement which created a certain amount of confusion and anxiety for the innkeepers. Pavel played his role magnificently.

On another one of Pavel's visits, he drew a wonderful caricature of Anton. Anton was doing some editorial work for Suvorin at the time. He had got Suvorin to publish the novels of Eugène Sue (*The Wandering Jew*) and Alexandre Dumas (*The Count of Monte Cristo, The Three Musketeers,* and others), but Anton insisted that these novels—especially those by Dumas—should be printed in an abridged form. He felt that parts unnecessarily exhausted the reader without advancing the story and, since they only made the book more expensive, he thought they should be cut. Suvorin agreed but doubted that he would be able to find a person qualified to make such cuts, so Anton volunteered.

The books' 1850s and 1860s editions were sent to Anton in Melikhovo, and Anton began mercilessly chopping and slashing the texts, sometimes deleting entire pages. While Anton was seated on his Turkish divan, undertaking his "slaughtering of the innocents," the sweet-natured Pavel parked himself in a quiet corner of the room and drew a caricature of him. In that drawing, Anton sits holding *The Count of Monte Cristo,* editing the book with his pencil, while Alexandre Dumas stands behind him, crying bitter tears. Anton Pavlovich carefully kept this drawing in his papers, but at some point it disappeared.

During one of Pavel's visits to Melikhovo, my brother finished a short novel that he later published as *The Story of an Unknown Man.*[13] For a long time, however, he could not decide whether or not to send it to publishers; he sent it out only after reading it aloud to Pavel. I remember this reading well: it was in the garden, during the day, and Pavel kept a very serious expression on his face as he listened and commented. At first, Anton had called it *My Patient's Story,* but Pavel suggested the new title, which stuck. That reading surprised me, because Anton never read his pieces to anyone and criticized authors who did.

During another one of Pavel's visits to Luka, a young professor from Kharkov University named V. F. Timofeev was staying with the Lintvariovs. He had just returned from a trip abroad and did an excellent impersonation of a German professor. He was a cheerful and jovial young man with whom Anton Pavlovich liked to drink. This excessive drinking did not sit at all well with the Lintvariovs, who feared having vodka in their house like the plague. I am sure that had Timofeev been a more regular visitor, he and Anton Pavlovich would have become really good friends.

Once Pavel, Anton, Timofeev, and I went to the Psiol to swim. When Timofeev took off his shoes, we were surprised to see that one of his heels was dark yellow. I am not sure if he had applied iodine to it or if he had been born like this. As soon as Anton noticed it, he asked the professor very seriously, "Vladimir Fiodorovich, when you smoke, how far do you keep the cigarette from your heel?" We all burst out laughing, especially Pavel.

Shortly before his death Pavel came to Melikhovo again and left us with some wonderful memories of that visit. He loved us all very deeply and was always saying how being with us was like being with his own family. Toward the end of his life, he became especially gentle and affectionate. He would bring along his son Misha, who took after his father in both looks and talent. He came to a sad end, however. When he was still a student his body was found in a stairway of a building, where he had shot himself outside the door of a woman he loved. Pavel later died of a heart attack in the fall of 1892 on the stage of the Mikhailovsky Theater in Saint Petersburg. He died in full costume and makeup, during a performance of Ostrovsky's comedy *Jokers*.

A revised version of Anton's play *Ivanov*, which I mentioned before, opened in Saint Petersburg in 1889. The original version had premiered in the Korsh Theater in Moscow on November 19, 1887. Anton had never intended to write it, in fact, but an opportunity he could not pass up presented itself.

Anton had run into Korsh in the lobby of his theater one night and they started talking about plays in general. At that time, serious plays were not popular, and Korsh's company performed mostly light comedies and vaudevilles. Knowing that Anton was a humorist, Korsh asked him whether he would write a play for his company. Korsh offered generous terms, so Anton sat down and began to write.

He wrote one act after another in the gloomy study at the Korneev house on Kudrinskaya-Sadovaya. The minute he finished an act, he would send it over to Korsh for a censorship review so the rehearsals could begin as soon as possible.

In spite of its hasty execution, *Ivanov* attracted widespread attention right from the beginning. Moscow society turned out in full for the sold-out opening night. Some were expecting the play to be a comical farce in the style of the short stories Anton had been publishing in *Fragments*, but it was actually quite serious.

As a result *Ivanov* turned out to be a mixed success. Many audience members applauded loudly and called for the author to take a bow. But overall, the play was not well understood. Long afterward, reviewers kept returning to and questioning the personality and character of the protagonist. The play nonetheless got people talking. It attracted attention for its dramatic style and the novelty of the story, and thus was Anton's life as a playwright launched.

Right after it opened, Anton wrote a letter to our brother Alexander saying, "You cannot imagine what happened. Out of this insignificant speck of shit, my little play, came the devil knows what. The audience shouted, clamored over each other, hushed each other, applauded. Somebody almost got into a fistfight in the cafeteria and in the gallery the students wanted to throw someone out, so the police had to come and remove two men. But the general excitement was pervasive. Sister almost fainted. Dyukovsky, who suddenly felt heart palpitations, simply fled, and Kiseliov, for no reason at all, grabbed his head and yelled, very believably, 'What am I to do now?!' The actors were all nervous and tense. The next day the *Moscow Leaflet* had a review by Piotr Kicheev, who called my play impudently cynical and immoral rubbish."[14]

I was present that first night and remember what took place in Korsh's theater. It was incredible. The audience members were jumping out of their seats and applauding. Some people were trying to quiet the crowd, some were whistling, and others were stomping their feet. The chairs and armchairs on the orchestra floor got moved around during the commotion, mixing up the rows and aisles so much that it was impossible to find one's seat. Those audience members in the boxes were quite alarmed and weren't sure whether to stay or go. A fight sprung up in the gallery between those shushing and those applauding. It is hardly surprising that two weeks after the performance, Anton wrote the following from Saint Petersburg: "If Korsh removes my play from the repertory, so much the better. Why embarrass myself? Let them go to hell."

The day after the aforementioned performance, Anton was visited at his apartment by Victor Alexandrov-Krylov,[15] whose plays made up the backbone of the Maly Theater's repertory at the time. He had come to offer my brother his services because he saw originality in *Ivanov* and was anticipating further success for the play. He would correct the play, change a few things, add some others, but on the condition that he would be a coauthor and get half of the royalties. Anton felt quite indignant, but he managed to decline politely.

Later, after Anton's famous one-act *The Bear*[16] had been performed all over the country, Krylov happened to publish a play called *The Bear Proposed*. It could not have been a coincidence. Anton, laughing, told us that Krylov had recently gone to a young local playwright to get help livening up his own play. After the playwright had finished his work, Krylov paid him only ten rubles. The playwright was so insulted that he became hysterical. "I will throw this money into his ugly face!" he fumed. Another playwright who happened to be there, V. A. Tikhonov, gravely suggested, "This money is bad—we must spend it on drink right away."

At the same time as *Ivanov*, Korsh was running a very funny play called *In the Caucus Mountains*, by Ivan Shcheglov.[17] His book, *The Gordian Knot*, had also just come out. Anton and I both liked the play and the book very much; there was something fresh and youthful about them.

Imagine how surprised we were to learn later that "Ivan Shcheglov" was really Ivan Leontievich Leontiev, a retired army captain who had served in the Turkish War and fought in many battles.

Anton Pavlovich became friends with him, and "Jean" (as Anton nicknamed him) soon became a frequent visitor. He was an effeminate man, affectionate, with a high-pitched laugh, like that of a hysterical girl. He had a real literary gift, but after the success of *In the Caucus Mountains,* he put all his energy into theater. His visits to us in Moscow were always welcome; he was always so sweet and nice that it was impossible to dislike him. He was also quite sentimental and would send our Mother postcards with flowery pictures and indecipherable handwriting. He sent her a card for every birthday and special occasion. Anton Pavlovich gave him a hard time about his weak spot for theater, but despite his gentle demeanor, Jean Shcheglov was intractable. The theater destroyed him in the end, though; his next few plays were unsuccessful and, growing dejected, he died in the prime of his life.

It was Jean Shcheglov who nicknamed Anton "Potiomkin" because of his great literary success.[18] Anton would occasionally sign his letters with this nickname. Jean's tenderness and fragility always touched Anton, and he would sometimes end his letters to him with: "Shaking your little goldfinch claw."[19] Indeed, there was something in Shcheglov's appearance and personality that made one think of a bird.

Around this same time, the Maly Theater in Moscow was staging a hugely successful drama called *The Second Youth* by P. M. Nevezhin.[20] The play was a melodramatic pastiche, but starring such luminaries as Fedotova, Leshkovskaya, Yuzhin, and Rybakov.[21] The play went for the jugular, and would leave the audience crying hysterically, especially when Yuzhin, playing a young son who had shot his father's mistress, came out on stage in shackles to say goodbye to his mother, played by Fedotova. The play brought in a lot of money.

Once during a performance of *The Second Youth,* Anton Pavlovich and Nevezhin ran into each other in the theater's foyer. They talked about *Ivanov* and *The Second Youth.* "Scribbling anything else these days?" asked the old playwright condescendingly of young Chekhov. "And you? What are you scribbling these days?" responded Anton in turn. To that, Nevezhin answered proudly: "After *The Second Youth,* is there anything else one can write?"

I met Nevezhin more than once. He had switched to writing literature and often brought his novels to me. "Just read it!" he would insist. "Such an interesting novel! You won't be able to put it down! A wonderful novel! You'll be delirious with joy!"

I would like to go into some detail about F. A. Korsh. He was a barrister who got his start in the theater by working for a Moscow entrepreneur named Madame Brenko. Anton once joked that her last name came from the German word *brennen,* which means "to burn down."[22] Soon after the Pushkin monument had been installed in Tverskaya Square, the Malkiel Brothers had a big building with a theater in it built there. (There actually was a funny song about the brothers that went something like this: "On Tverskaya, on the square, whose is that building, big and square? On Neglinnaya, on the street, whose is that building big and sleek?") It was the first private theater in Moscow after the imperial monopoly of theaters was rescinded in 1882. In fact, the theater's official name was the Theater near the Pushkin Monument.

Madame Brenko leased the theater; hired the best provincial actors, including Ivanov-Kozelsky, Pisarev, Andreev-Burlak; and produced a diverse repertory of shows, from *Will-o'-the-wisp* by Antropov to *The Forest* to *Hamlet* to *Fallen Rome.*[23] In spite of her diligent production work, however, Madame Brenko still went bankrupt.

In contrast, F. A. Korsh was single-handedly renting the theater's coatroom, but doing very well with it. Even though Madame Brenko had to give out complimentary tickets to fill the house, each member of the audience still had to pay twenty kopecks to put his coat in the coatroom. So no matter how few audience members paid to see the show, Korsh still made a profit. After Madame Brenko went bankrupt, the actors' cooperative moved to Lianozov's theater in Gazetny Alley. Korsh moved with them and continued to operate the coatroom until he eventually took over the entire business.

In fact, after he became the owner, Korsh used the coatroom to save the company. The daily expenses of running the theater accounted for approximately one-third of the ticket receipts from a full house. When the house was full, the coatroom alone brought in the exact amount needed to run the theater. So Korsh decided to send complimentary tickets to schools and universities to bring in younger people and to keep the theater full. Of course, every student was glad to go and see a theater show for the price of the coat check. So the coatroom offset all the expenses for the night, while the paying customers made Korsh his profit.

Korsh was a passionate admirer of the theater; he wrote and translated such plays as *Matchmaker, The Struggle for Survival, Madame Saint-Jean,* and finally decided to build his own theater in Moscow. I don't remember who helped him build it, but I do remember that it was finished unusually quickly. The construction workers worked day and night using electrical arc lights so that the theater could open by August 16.

When the theater finally opened in 1882, it smelled dank and there were leaks in the walls; it was obvious that the construction had been rushed. The actors made up for it though. The hand-picked troupe consisted of Gradov-Sokolov, Solonin, Svetlov, the famous V. N. Davydov, Glama-Meshcherskaya, Rybchinskaya, Martynova, Kosheva, and Krasovskaya.[24] Those actors together made up an exceptional comedic ensemble, and comedy was the staple of Korsh's repertory. But the actors were more than just comedians and their names are part of general theater history. The artist A. S. Yanov was the designer; his spectacular sets beguiled audiences. For a show based on Turgenev's *A Night in Sorrento,* he recreated Naples on the stage. There were the shimmering lights along the promenade and on boats and ships lying at anchor, Mount Vesuvius with smoke coming out of its top, and the moon reflecting in the bay. By the time K. S. Shilovsky sang "Si tu m'aimais," the audience was going crazy.

The Korsh Theater became one of the most popular theaters in Moscow. A brochure celebrating the theater's tenth anniversary I found at our Melikhovo house claimed that the theater had been visited by more than 1.5 million spectators and had produced more than 500 plays. Korsh introduced the Russian public to plays by Sardou, Pailleron, Daudet,[25] and other outstanding foreign playwrights whose works could not be seen in any other theater. His main achievement, however, was the creation of general-admission matinees for the classical plays, which were very popular and well-attended by young people, and was a concept many provincial theaters in Russia later imitated.

VII

RECOGNITION

LET ME RETURN TO OUR TIME IN LUKA. OUR FAMILY also spent the summer of 1889 there, but it was not as merry or cheerful a time as the year before. Our circle of friends expanded, and in addition to our family, two other interesting men were staying with the Lintvariovs that summer—the well-known economist Vassily Pavlovich Vorontsov and the legal expert A. Y. Efimenko. But a very sad event cast a long shadow over our family that summer—my brother Nikolay, the artist, died.[1]

The news of Nikolay's death reached Anton while he was traveling. He was looking to purchase an estate that would be his primary residence and there were some for sale in Sorochintsy and in a few towns in Poltava province. The towns were exactly the way Gogol had portrayed them in his stories. After Anton heard the news, he wrote a letter to our brother Alexander saying, "The night sky was gray and it was raining hard when we arrived at the

Lintvariovs' relative's house in the village of Bokumovka, in Poltava province. Still drenched and chilled, we went to our cold beds and fell asleep to the sound of the rain drumming on the roof. In the morning the weather was the same—it felt like the weather in Vologda. We had barely woken up when a peasant from Mirgorod knocked on the door and handed us a soaked telegram. It said simply, 'Kolia passed.' We rode our horses back to the station to catch a train. There were eight-hour delays at each station along the way. Our family had never known death before; for the first time we saw a coffin in our home."

The funeral was very basic. Anton was distraught and left Luka soon after the funeral to wander around. He almost went abroad, but then changed his mind. He got stuck in Odessa for some reason. The Maly Theater Company happened to be there on tour at the same time and he met the young actress "Glafirochka" Panova[2] who had switched from ballet to drama, and whom he apparently liked. Later in Moscow, the actor Lensky's[3] wife tried to act as a matchmaker between them, but Anton was very difficult to manage in those kinds of situations, and she soon abandoned the idea. It was not until Anton settled in Yalta that his drifting phase finally came to an end.

After Nikolay's death, a strange apathy descended over Anton, and he lost interest in everything. It took two months for him to regain his confidence in himself and in his writing. Only then, living in the Korneev house on Kudrinskaya-Sadovaya, did he recommence his work, and at a feverish pace. During that time he wrote "A Dull Story"[4] and his play *The Wood Demon*,[5] which was produced in Solovtsov and Abramova's theater on December 27, 1889.[6] He also began the painstaking work of collecting supplies for an upcoming trip to the island of Sakhalin, in the North Pacific. But I will go into more detail about this trip later.

Anton left Odessa for Yalta in the summer of 1889 without any definitive plans, but ended up living there for a fairly long time. Once, as he was strolling down a Yalta street past someone's summer house, the gate opened and three very well-dressed young ladies came out. One of them said aloud to herself within my brother's earshot, "There is the writer Chekhov." Their cosmopolitan style had caught Anton Pavlovich's eye. When he saw them again in the city park, they finally made each other's acquaintance. It turned out that the ladies were the Shavrov sisters, Kharkov landowners who lived permanently in Saint Petersburg, but came to Crimea every summer.

Their familiarity lasted beyond the vacation. One evening, in Moscow, Anton Pavlovich received a perfumed letter sent through a servant girl. It was from Madame Shavrov, the mother of the young ladies, informing him that the entire family had just moved from Saint Petersburg to Moscow, and asking him to renew the acquaintanceship that had begun so opportunely in Yalta.

The Shavrov ladies read a lot and knew all the latest books by both Russian and foreign writers very well; they had even read the foreign books in their original languages. I, on the other hand, knew foreign literature only through

bad translations and was usually embarrassed to have conversations about such books. That embarrassment spurred
me to study foreign languages. After I mastered English,
French, and Italian, I became a translator myself.

The eldest sister, Elena Mikhailovna,[7] turned out to be
a writer, and Anton occasionally helped her place her pieces
for publication. He thought she was very gifted and recommended that she develop her writing as much as possible. But being a typical woman of her circle, having no need
to earn money to survive, she did not attach much importance to her talent. She signed her pieces with the name
"Shastunov" and maintained a correspondence with Anton.
His letters to her were included in the collection published
by our sister Maria Pavlovna, but because this talented
young woman wished to remain anonymous, the letters appear in the book under the initials "E. M. Sh." Anton tried
to help her short stories get published and often succeeded,
but he always rebuked her for not cultivating her talent by
writing more. He would frequently breakfast with her in
Bolshaya Moskovskaya or in the Hermitage on his trips
from Melikhovo to Moscow for business. She called him
her *chèr maître,* and he usually signed his letters with that
nickname. She was also a wonderful singer, and her photograph hung in the study of the Yalta house for many years.
There was something special about her, and their friendship was strong and long-lasting.

Her sister, Olga Mikhailovna, became a well-known actress in classical plays in spite of the fact that acting was
frowned upon for a woman of her background. Her stage

name was Darskaya. When Anton Pavlovich learned that she had become an actress (which was a complete surprise to all of us), he expressed his sincere approval and said, "Good for her!" Later, when Anton Pavlovich lived in Melikhovo and needed to raise funds to build schools, both sisters offered their help. They came to Serpukhov from Moscow and put on an amateur theater show, dazzling the local audience with the splendor of their dresses, the glitter of their diamonds, and their talented performances.

In 1889, Anton became more deeply involved with the theater. The actor N. Solovtsov, who worked at the Korsh Theater and had been very successful in Chekhov's play *The Bear,* left Korsh's company and opened his own house on Theater Square in Moscow with the actress Abramova. But business was slow because there were no good plays to produce—even during such usually lucrative periods as Christmas and Shrovetide. In order to fill the house, they needed a noteworthy play. So Solovtsov went to Anton and asked, "Please support us, Anton Pavlovich, give us a play."

With only ten or twelve days left until Christmas, Solovtsov made Anton the tempting offer of 1,000 rubles for a play. Anton thus began work on *The Wood Demon.* Every day he would write a new act and I would make two handwritten copies of it. Solovtsov would pick them up and send them, via the conductor of an overnight train, to Saint Petersburg for the censor's review. The work went quickly—Anton wrote, Solovtsov hurried him, and I copied. As a result, the play was completed on deadline, ran for a few performances, and Anton received his money.

Solovtsov still lost money however, and Anton was fairly unhappy with the results.

It would have been impossible to be happy with it. *The Wood Demon* was written in a hurry and Solovtsov did a horrible job with the production. The actress M. N. G.,[8] who was fairly overweight, took the role of a young girl, the first ingénue. The actor Roshchin-Insarov[9] played her lover and could not even embrace her properly. Then the effect of the wildfire in the woods was done so poorly that the audience could not help but giggle. The one saving grace was that the actor Zubov,[10] who had been the star of the Abramova theater, did a wonderful job.

Anton pulled the play from the theater's repertory right away and kept it in his desk for a long time. It took him a few years to revisit it. Then, in 1896, he completely rewrote the play, giving it a new structure and changing the name to *Uncle Vanya*.

MEANWHILE, Anton had been suffering from coughing fits for some time, especially at night. That cough paved the way for tuberculosis later on, but my brother did not wish to pay attention to it or to take better care of himself. He first started coughing up blood in 1884, when he was reporting on the Rykov trial in Moscow for the *Saint Petersburg Gazette*.

The trial took place in Moscow, but was about a small provincial town called Skopin, in Ryazan province. The defendant was a merchant named Rykov who had been operating a bank. He advertised huge interest rates on deposits, and village priests, deacons, and government officers from all over Russia hurried to invest their savings.

The bank was soon handling millions. Rykov was elected mayor and turned Skopin into a decent town through his improvements. Everybody trusted him; the bank's board of directors listened to him without question; and everything was going very well—until, that is, the great princes and governors began borrowing money and defaulting on their loans. Although Rykov received medals and honors from them, there was not enough money to run the bank. The bank crashed and Rykov, along with his board of directors and his accountants, ended up in court.

The prosecution accused Rykov of being the main embezzler since he was the one eating lobsters and drinking champagne. He tried to explain who ruined the bank and squandered the money, but to no avail and was locked up under guard in the courthouse jail. During the two-week trial, Anton was dispatched to the courthouse literally day and night, and continued writing for the newspapers even at home. His first symptoms of tuberculosis appeared under the strain of this work.

Our family did not understand the seriousness of his illness until years later, in Melikhovo. We had to take him to a clinic in Moscow almost by force just to get him treatment. The influenza that swept through Moscow in 1888 was especially hard on him. But even then, he would

not allow doctors to listen to his lungs and make a correct diagnosis.

Anton coughed particularly violently during the period that we lived on Kudrinskaya-Sadovaya from the fall
of 1886 to the spring of 1890. Our narrow two-story rental
there had an unusual layout. Anton's bedroom and study,
my room, the main stairway, the kitchen, and two rooms
for the servants were all on the ground floor. The drawing
room, two rooms for our Mother and sister, the dining
room, and another room with a skylight were on the second floor. My responsibility before bed was to light the
lamp in Anton's bedroom because he often woke up and
did not like to be in the dark. Only a thin partition separated our rooms, and we used to talk through it whenever
we were unable to sleep in the middle of the night. It was
through that wall that I was able to hear how bad his
cough was.

Anton could not be alone during that period, and as I
mentioned before, our house was always filled with young
people playing the piano, singing, joking, and laughing upstairs. He would write at his desk downstairs, energized by
the noise. He always shared in our fun and thrived on the
excitement.

We first met Lika Mizinova at that house, through
Maria and her job as a schoolteacher. One day Maria
showed up with Lika, a modest and shy girl of about eighteen. My sister walked through the door and announced,
"Look, I've brought a pretty girl here for you." We must

have made Lika quite uncomfortable when we surrounded her but as soon as we began joking and talking, she seemed to warm up. We all liked her very much. It was strange to think that she was a schoolteacher; it seemed like no student would ever listen to such a shy girl. We didn't think we would see her again, but she came back for another visit. When she arrived, we all gathered on top of the stairway to look at her. She was so embarrassed by the attention that she buried her face in the fur coats hanging on the rack.

Anton used to call her "Lika the Beautiful." Indeed, she was endowed with a rare beauty, both in her appearance and in her personality. People always stared at her but she never exhibited the slightest hint of vanity. In addition to beauty, nature had given her intelligence and a merry disposition. She was witty and could easily parry a provocative remark, so her responses during our playful banter were always fun to hear. All of my brothers treated her like a sister, although I think Anton was interested in her. She was one of our most welcome guests, and her arrival always lightened the mood. Maria Pavlovna introduced her to new people by saying, "This is my brother's friend, and mine." Our Father loved her like his own daughter, and she was one of our closest confidants. Anton's friends were all infatuated with her. Of course, the artist Levitan professed his love, and the writer Ignaty Potapenko was seriously interested in her. I will talk about Lika more later, as she truly did become like a member of our family.

THE house on Kudrinskaya-Sadovaya must have felt proud to have welcomed so many famous people. I already mentioned Grigorovich and Tchaikovsky's visits. The magnificent actor A. P. Lensky of the Maly Theater not only visited us as a guest, he also graced us with performances. Before his first public performance of Shakespeare's *Richard III*, Lensky performed his role for us in our drawing room. Lensky and the actress M. N. Ermolova (whom I mentioned earlier) were Moscow's favorite stars at the time. They always performed together and were both first-class actors. It would have been unthinkable to produce the classical plays without them. I was lucky enough to have seen M. N. Ermolova on stage at the Popular Theater on Solianka in 1876 at the very beginning of her theatrical career.

Ermolova, Lensky, and Yuzhin were absolutely inimitable in Victor Hugo's play *Hernani*. The play captivated Moscow in 1889 and it was all people talked about. It had to be produced as *Gernani* because the censor had deemed it unacceptable for Russian theaters. To avoid any trouble with the government, the theater gave no indication that the play was by Victor Hugo, but even so the show sold out and it was nearly impossible to get in.

V. N. Davydov, the star of both the Korsh and Alexandrinsky Theaters, also visited our house on Kudrinskaya-Sadovaya. He was truly an extraordinary man. Despite his obesity, he was remarkably agile. When he imitated a ballerina dancing her most intricate *pas*, you almost forgot that you were looking at a fat middle-aged man. Davydov read us Tolstoy's recently published *The Power of Darkness*,[11] performing all of the characters. He changed his voice for each character and his rendition of the role of the young girl Anyutka was quite unforgettable. Davydov was also an incomparable storyteller, especially on the subject of provincial actors. He could act out all the characters of his stories so well that even the most indifferent person would be doubled over in laughter.

It was also thanks to him that Anton's one-act *The Swan Song* was created.[12] I was very familiar with this one-act from writing copies of it, but—good gracious!—how many new "gags" it had acquired from Davydov! He improvised about Mochalov and about Shchepkin and about other actors, so one could barely recognize Anton's original. But it was so enjoyable and was performed with such great talent that Anton was not offended. Davydov had also played the main character in *Ivanov* at the Korsh Theater in 1887.

Another guest of that house was N. A. Leikin, the publisher of *Fragments*.[13] He was short, broad-shouldered, lame in one leg, and eccentric. Since he himself was extremely hospitable, he always expected to be treated like an important guest. He liked relaxing in good company and could spend hours at the table. He also liked to drink heavily around friends. After a big supper, no matter how filling it was, he would still send a servant to bring him *uglitsky*, a type of smoked sausage that I found disgusting but which he ate with gusto. Leikin was a man of

many talents. His forefathers were simple peasants from
the Yaroslavl province but he was brought to Saint Petersburg as a child and given as an apprentice to a shop
owner. Thanks to his gifts he advanced quickly, became a
writer, then a property owner, then a member of the city
council, and finally one of the heads of the City Credit
Society. He had written, by his own account, more than
20,000 short stories and sketches, and called himself "a
man of letters" with great pride. The doors of his house
on Dvoriansky Street were always open to everyone, and
he loved indulging his friends.

Leikin always listed the price of things to try to show
his guests how much he liked them, and how generously
they were being treated. "Please eat this smoked fish; it
cost two rubles and seventy-five kopecks a pound. Now
drink this marsala, I paid two rubles and eighty kopecks a
bottle for it. And these sardines are not the forty-five-
kopeck ones—no, they cost sixty kopecks a can!" He did
not have children and lived with his spouse, Praskovia
Nikiforovna. He bought a huge estate with a real palace for
just the two of them. It was located on the Neva River and
he bought it from Count Stroganov. When Anton came to
visit him there, he was surprised by its grandeur and asked,
"You practically live alone, why do you need all of this rubbish?" Leikin answered: "All this used to be owned by
counts. Now Leikin the boor owns it."

The last time I saw him was in Saint Petersburg, after
Anton's death. It was at a banquet organized to honor the
French press corps during the visit of President Loubet

and the French navy to Saint Petersburg. Thumping his chest, with tears in his eyes, Leikin said, "I gave birth to Chekhov!" This enormous banquet took place at The Bear, a restaurant on Bolshaya Konyushenaya Street, with more than 1,000 people present. Among the pompous guests were representatives of the French press who had accompanied President Loubet to Saint Petersburg to trump up a French-Russian alliance and to boost the appropriate positive mood. Among the journalists was Gaston Calmette,[14] editor of the newspaper *Le Figaro*. The French journalists had all been awarded Russian medals and were wearing them that evening, which made for a somewhat comical sight, given the fact that the decoration they had been given, the Order of Saint Stanislav of the Third Degree, was one that even a petty government official in Russia would have been embarrassed to wear. For some reason, the organizers were being stingy with the awards. For example, Calmette himself only received the Order of Saint Anna, although he too seemed quite happy with it.

The organizers' intention was to put on a nice show and have the French experience true Russian hospitality. The guests were offered supper and entertainment. Kschesinsskaya danced, Vialtseva sang and glittered with diamonds, the Gypsy chorus raved and raged.[15] Caviar, sturgeon, *balyk,* red-beet borscht, and other gluttonous examples of our national fare were in abundance. Both sides gave speeches, and Suvorin, who had been elected the chairman of the event, addressed the guests in French.

They toasted Russia and France, the press, and so on. One of the Russian guests tapped the table with his cane until it got quiet and said to the crowd, "I am raising this glass to A. S. Suvorin and Madame Angot!"

"To whom?" asked Suvorin, who had missed the remark. "To A. S. Suvorin and to Madame Adan!" the writer corrected himself.[16] At that moment, the orchestra, not knowing what to do, started playing a flourish. The Russians all felt awkward, but the French, not having understood a word, applauded. The tension dissipated as soon as the Gypsies started howling and stomping their feet, drowning out the Russian and French voices.

I believe it was Leikin who introduced us to the writer N. S. Leskov.[17] Already an old man by that time, he had gray hair and wore an expression of sad resignation on his face. He brought an autographed copy of his book *The Steel Flea* as a gift for Anton. We knew his writing from his novels *Cathedral Folk* and *The Sealed Angel,* which we liked a lot. We thought *Little Things from the Lives of Bishops* was funny, but *Nowhere* and *At Daggers Drawn* definitely disappointed us. The latter two novels alienated his readers, ruined his reputation, and placed poor Leskov alongside right-wing reactionaries. With the passage of time, however, he came to acknowledge his mistakes, and sincerely regretted writing those novels. During his visit with Anton, his eyes welled up with tears and he said very touchingly, "You are a young writer, and I am already old. When you write, write only the good, the honest, and the kind, so that later in your old age, you won't have anything to regret, the way I do now."

By that time, he believed in pacifism and had become a vegetarian. With his gentle and endearing manners, Leskov left a very affecting impression on us.

᠅   ᠅

THE editorial office of the magazine *Artist* was located across the street from our house on Kudrinskaya-Sadovaya. F. A. Kumanin, the publisher, was a tall, large man who made a whistling sound when he spoke. Anton nicknamed him "The Wheezer." The magazine published my brother's plays *The Bear, The Proposal,*[18] and others. My own two vaudevilles were published there as well. It was an elegant magazine in those days, attracting the best talent available, including Tatiana Lvovna Shchepkina-Kupernik, whose first dramatic piece, *A Summer Picture,* was published there. I do not know for sure whether or not my brother and sister knew her before, but I had the pleasure of meeting her through Kumanin.

Tatiana was a tiny, vivacious, and interesting young girl, with a very quick wit. I was studying foreign languages then, and Lika Mizinova had nicknamed me "English Grammar" because I always carried a textbook with me. What amazed me right away about Tatiana Lvovna, who was still quite young at that time, was her thorough knowledge of languages. She became a frequent visitor to our house in Moscow, and later in Melikhovo as well.

As she began publishing her work, her talent grew. She translated Molière and Edmond Rostand, as well as writing her own stories. I can personally attest from my travels all over Russia that young people throughout the country adored her writings and knew her poems by heart. I remember how excited the public was about her translation of Rostand's play *The Princess Far Away,* and it went on to be staged in Moscow, Saint Petersburg, and in the best provincial theaters. Entire soliloquies from the play were recited publicly and songs were written using the play's lyrics. She also authored several original dramas that were successfully performed in both capital cities. During one of her visits to Melikhovo, Tatiana and Anton became godparents to the daughter of our neighbors, the Shakhovskoys. After that, Anton always called her "Godmother."

Tania introduced me to the actress L. B. Yavorskaya. Although I was never a fan of her work and disliked her voice—to me it always sounded like she had a sore throat—she was an intelligent woman and quite progressive. She always chose liberal-leaning plays for her benefit performances, had many fans among the young, and possessed good taste in literature. She was very popular at Korsh's Theater in Moscow and at Suvorin's in Saint Petersburg.

THERE was a period of Anton's life when his work in *Russian Thought* brought him into contact with two members

of the editorial board, M. A. Sablin and V. A. Goltsev. Ignaty Potapenko was also friends with them, and we all
spent a few nights at Testov's and at the Hermitage Restaurant with Lika the Beautiful, my sister, Tanechka Kupernik,
and a few others. Those were wonderful and unforgettable
evenings. Anton and Potapenko's quips were inexhaustible,
and Goltsev made drunken speeches, always beginning
them with "Allow me, a bald Russian liberal . . ."

❧   ❧

WHILE Anton was in the midst of writing *The Steppe*,[19]
A. N. Pleshcheev wrote him a letter about a friend who was
a remarkably talented critic, but too timid to submit his
writing to the press. We soon had a visit from an elderly
but still red-headed man who introduced himself as Piotr
Nikolaevich Ostrovsky. He was the brother of the famous
playwright A. N. Ostrovsky[20] and lived on Novinsky Boulevard. Anton invited him to sit and they started talking
about literature. I was there, too, and found the conversation very interesting.

After Piotr Nikolaevich left, having filled the room
with cheap cigar smoke, my brother said, "What a remarkable critic! How many civilizations vanished, and
great pieces of art, too, simply because there were no good
critics around!"

Anton sent him the finished manuscript of *The Steppe*
to get his opinion. He did not come into the house when he
dropped off the manuscript along with a thick letter; he
just left the papers at the door. He must have felt awkward

about his extensive critique of *The Steppe,* but Anton appreciated his straightforward manner.

Speaking of the Ostrovskys, Alexander and Piotr's eldest brother was Mikhail Nikolaevich Ostrovsky, who was the secretary of state property and a typical Saint Petersburg functionary. Anton liked to tell the following anecdote about him:

> After the opening night of one of his plays in the Alexandrinsky Theater, the playwright Ostrovsky celebrated with the actors all night long. Early in the morning, on his way home after the long night, he suddenly decided to pay his brother, the secretary of state property in Saint Petersburg, a visit at his office. The receptionist brought the playwright, who had spent the entire night drinking, into the office. Without looking up from his desk, the secretary pointed to the chair for his brother to sit in, and continued signing papers.
>
> "Misha," began the playwright, "What a great binge we had! Gorbunov improvised a monologue; wow, it was so great. Another actor's stories were so funny my sides are still aching. And then we went to the Gypsies! And then the company went to Novaya Derevnia. We stopped at an inn and drank a bowl of brine each so we would not feel sick—" The secretary suddenly raised his head, leaned back in his seat, threw his pen down and, interrupting his brother, exclaimed, "I don't see any-

thing good in it, Sasha!" The playwright got up and said reprovingly, "And you think these papers of yours are better?" And the brothers parted.

I must not forget to mention another memorable meeting that took place in the Korneev house. One day, our family was upstairs finishing dinner when the doorbell rang. Masha had been expecting someone, so she got up from the table and started walking toward the stairs. I ran ahead of her and opened the door to a man of medium height sporting a broad, thick beard. "I am Korolenko," he said.[21]

Oh my God! Korolenko! What a surprise! We had all known his writing for a long time, and I knew his work *Makar's Dream* almost by heart! Just then, Anton appeared and all three of us went into the study.

It happens sometimes that strangers get along well from the very first moment they meet, and such was the case that night. Korolenko enchanted us with his simplicity, sincerity, modesty, and intelligence. We started talking, and I was riveted as he told us about his time in Siberia. After many years of exile, he finally got permission to return to Russia and boarded the train in Tyumen. He was so overcome with emotion when he saw the train car that he started sobbing in front of everybody. "I cried and cried," he said. "The other passengers thought it was from grief, but no—it was from joy."

He stayed with us all night. Anton invited him upstairs, where our Mother and sister prepared tea, and we continued listening to his stories.

Korolenko went to visit my brother in Yalta, too. It was after Maxim Gorky's election to the Academy of Science had been annulled, and they were discussing a plan to make other honorary academics leave the academy in protest. I think they met in Nizhny Novgorod and Saint Petersburg as well. I deeply regret that I never had another opportunity to see this remarkable man. But I will always remember the day I met him.

VIII

ANTON'S
TRAVELS

In July 1890, Anton visited Sakhalin Island, in the North Pacific.[1] The trip came about completely by chance and he made the decision to go to the Far East so suddenly that we didn't know whether or not to take him seriously at first.

The year before, I had been preparing for the post-university state examination, for which I had had to review my lecture notes on criminal law. I came across some interesting sections on the penal colony and labor camps on Sakhalin Island, and these notes piqued my brother's interest. He started reading them too and was soon planning a trip there. Not wanting to go to the island unprepared, he started gathering information. He obtained some rare books about Sakhalin from the Rumiantsev Library and put our sister and her girlfriends to work taking notes and copying excerpts for him.

He was concerned that because he was a writer, the local administration would only show him what they wanted him to see. He went to Saint Petersburg to petition the head of the administration of prisons for an all-access pass in January of 1890. It was a delicate matter, because at the same time he didn't want his trip to seem officially sanctioned. Anyway, his request was denied. He finally began his journey in April with only a reporter's identification in his pocket. We gathered at the station to see him off to Yaroslavl. Our friend Dimitry Pavlovich Kuvshinnikov placed a bottle of cognac in a special leather case over Anton's shoulder with the strict order to drink it only on the shores of the Pacific Ocean—which was precisely what Anton did.

Spring had come late that year and it was still quite cold. Anton traveled along the Volga and Kama Rivers to Perm. From there, he went to Tyumen by rail. The Great Siberian Railway did not yet exist, and he had to travel all the way through Siberia on coaches and riverboats. Despite having researched the island, Anton had still packed impractically. I had bought him an excellent but unwieldy suitcase. If he had had one made of leather—flat and soft— he could have lain on it while in the coach. He should have taken tea, sugar, and canned food with him, since it was impossible to find any of those in Siberia. He also should have taken an extra pair of felt boots with him, or at least had the ones he took fixed with leather. Our traveler encountered "monstrously cold" days and nights, overflowing rivers, limited access to food, mud so deep that to get through it he said he "did not ride but rather swam," as well as incongruous heat and suffocating smoke from immense forest fires. Luckily, his tuberculosis was not yet that advanced. Used to the simple life, Anton took it all in stride and faced the hardships in good spirits. While he was not sure that his journey would make a valuable contribution to science or literature, he hoped to have two or three days that he would remember—either with bitterness or excitement—all his life.

After a two-month journey full of unimaginable trials and deprivations, Anton finally reached Sakhalin on July 11. He lived there for more than three months, walking the entire island and conducting the first private census. He spoke personally to each of the 10,000 convicts, and learned every detail about their lives in detention.

Anton wrote to Suvorin with his reflections on his upcoming journey to Sakhalin, saying, "Sakhalin is a place of the most unbearable suffering that can befall a man, free or shackled. . . . I regret that I am not sentimental, or I would say that we need to pay homage to places like Sakhalin, the way the Turks do to Mecca . . . From the books that I've been reading, it's clear that we have let millions of people rot in prisons. We do it for no reason, without thinking, just like barbarians. Our country has forced people to walk in fetters in the cold for thousands of miles, infected them with syphilis, and dumped them all into the hands of red-nosed prison wardens. And now all of the educated people of Europe know that the wardens are not the only ones perpetuating these abuses—we all are."[2]

During Anton's absence, my own path brought me to a town called Aleksin, in Tula province, located on the banks of the Oka River. A tiny community of only 700 residents, it was graced with a remarkable climate and a magnificent countryside. The view from the river bluff was indescribable. Standing by the church, overlooking the river, I could see the ornate railroad bridge, the little village, and the road lined with birch trees running next to the train. Across the river, next to the station, a man named Kovrigin built three little summer-houses. One of those little houses would later play a role in our life.

On December 7, 1890, Anton was scheduled to return to Moscow on the express train at five o'clock in the afternoon. He had sent a telegram from Odessa asking the whole family to meet him. Since we had expected him on December 10, we had to meet him in Tula. Our Mother had been visiting me in Aleksin, so we went to see him together.

By the time we got to Tula, Anton's train had already arrived from the south, and he was in the middle of dinner with a Navy midshipman named Glinka and another man. The man had a very broad face, narrow eyes, and was dressed in out-of-fashion civilian clothes. It turned out that he was a priest from Sakhalin Island and his name was Irakly. He was Buryat, an ethnic minority from Siberia. Anton and Glinka each had a mongoose they had bought in India and the mongooses were standing on their hind legs, peering at their food. Between the strange-looking Sakhalin priest and the mongooses, their group really stood out. A curious crowd had gathered around their table and

you could hear people asking questions like, "Is that an Indian? Are those monkeys?"

After a warm reunion with Anton, Mother and I
boarded the car, and all five of us continued on our way to
Moscow. Anton had a cage with what we thought was a female mongoose in it. This creature, however, was both wild
and mean, and it turned out to be a palm cat, a mongoose-
like animal from Southeast Asia. The Hindu who had sold
it to Anton had swindled him.

We arrived in Moscow just as the streetlights were
coming on. As soon as our car stopped at the platform, a
lady stormed inside, screaming "Where is my son? Where
is my son?" and threw herself into Glinka's arms. It was his
mother, Baroness Ikskul, who had come from Saint Petersburg to meet him. From the station, we went home to
the Firgang house on Malaya Dmitrovka Street. The venerable Buryat came home with us. Once we arrived, we let
the mongoose off his leash and opened the door of the cage
containing the palm cat. The palm cat immediately hid
under the bookshelf and only ever came out at night to get
food. As for the mongoose, he felt right at home in
Moscow and immediately established himself as the master of the house. Endlessly curious, he would stand on his
hind legs and poke his pointy nose into every gap and opening. Nothing escaped his attention. He scraped out the dirt
between the planks of our wood floors, ripped off wallpa-
per in search of bugs, jumped into laps and put his nose into
people's glasses of tea, turned over book pages, and put his
paw into the inkwell. Two or three times, he stood up on

his hind legs trying to look into a burning lamp from the top. Left in a room alone, he grew lonely, but was happy again as soon as there were people around. He was just like a dog.

Unfortunately, living with a mongoose and a palm cat in a small apartment in the winter turned out to be very inconvenient. The mongoose launched fierce attacks on the palm cat, scared Anton's visitors, and ruined so many things during his hunting expeditions for flies and spiders that none of us could wait for the summer, when we could let the mongoose roam free. When a visitor left his hat or gloves on the hallway's windowsill, we could never be sure that the mongoose would not shred the gloves or do something impolite in the top hat.

The palm cat never got used to humans at all. She hid constantly, except when the floor polisher came. He worked barefoot and the cat would suddenly jump out from under the shelf and seize his foot. The poor man would drop his broom and wax, grab his foot, and scream "Damn cat! I hope you die!"

The apartment on Malaya Dmitrovka was very small and I sometimes had to sleep on the floor during my visits. Every so often in the middle of the night, I would feel the palm cat's sharp teeth biting my foot! She would come out from under the shelf, crawl under my blanket to get warm and bite me if I jerked in my sleep.

When we slept in the same room, Anton would share his impressions of Sakhalin with me at night. Three stories made a lasting impression on me. One was about a typhoon off the coast of China. My brother was on a steamship called *Petersburg* on his return trip. The ship did not have any cargo and was being wildly tossed by the wind and waves. The captain came to Anton and suggested that he keep his revolver ready in his pocket, just in case he needed to commit suicide when the ship started sinking. That revolver became a part of the display at the Chekhov Museum in Yalta.

Another story I remember was one about a French steamer that ran aground. Per international naval rules at the time, the *Petersburg* had to stop and assist. The seamen threw the French a line, but when our steamer started pulling, the line snapped in two. The second time, they managed to tie it on and pull the French ship to safety. Following behind the Russian ship the French shouted, "*Vive la Russie!*" and played the Russian national anthem until each ship went back to its own course. After the French ship was gone, the Russians remembered that they had forgotten to charge the French 1,000 rubles for the broken line (all rescue expenses were to be paid by the rescued party). The 1,000 rubles had to be split among those who signed the incident report, including my brother Anton.

The third story that stayed with me was about my brother bathing in the Indian Ocean. In order for him to bathe, the crew would throw a line down the ship's stern. Anton then had to dive off the bow, grab the line as it came past, and hold onto it while the ship kept moving. As soon as he got into the water to wash off, he saw pilot fish and a shark swimming toward him (this episode made it into his story "Gusev"[3]). The island of Ceylon, however, made up for all the difficulties, he said. It was a paradise on earth, an exotic fairy-tale setting where, according to Anton, a beautiful Indian woman fell in love with him.

After this amazing journey, Anton found life in Moscow boring. A few short days after his return he left to visit A. S. Suvorin in Saint Petersburg and from there they traveled abroad together. Anton had never been to Western Europe. Now he traveled to Vienna, Nice, Paris, Biarritz, and Naples, but it was "the blue-eyed Venice" that really exceeded his expectations. Venice's canals and gondolas, the San Marco Piazza, and the delightful evenings he spent there inspired in him a childlike wonder and excitement and made him confess (although he had already seen Ceylon, that heaven on earth) that he had "never seen anything like it. . . . One wishes to stay here forever," he wrote to our brother Ivan. While in Nice, he visited Monte Carlo and lost 900 francs at the roulette table, but he took it as a new life experience rather than a loss. He wrote to me about it, saying, "I am content with myself." Anton plunged into new experiences, the same way he had jumped off the moving steamer into the Indian Ocean. Next was a visit to Naples, where he climbed Mount Vesuvius, and after immersing himself in the culture in Paris, Anton Pavlovich finally headed home to Moscow.

While Anton was away travelling, it had come time to think about a house for the summer. It fell to me to find one near Aleksin "by any means," since spending the summer in Moscow would be unthinkable. After failing to locate a house on someone's estate and feeling pressed for time, I decided to rent one of the Kovrigin summer houses on the Oka River.

On May 3, only three days after his return from abroad, Anton came to Aleksin. Of course, he disliked the house I had rented. There was no fence around it; it sat bleakly at the edge of the forest; and we couldn't even go outside the first few days because of a very strong wind.

Once we had settled into the new place, we sent for Lika the Beautiful. She arrived on a steamship from Serpukhov with I. I. Levitan. To be honest, we did not have enough room for them both, but we made do, and the two guests improved the mood right away. Anton's witty remarks got the jokes and laughter flying and Levitan loved nothing better than to show off in front of the ladies.

On the steamer, Lika and Levitan had struck up a conversation with a young man who turned out to be E. D. Bylim-Kolosovsky, a local landowner. Bylim-Kolosovsky remembered that Lika had said she was headed to our place, and only a couple of days later sent over two carriages for us to come visit him. This promised to be a new experience, and we set out eagerly. The trip turned out to be both interesting and rather mysterious because we never actually saw Bylim-Kolosovsky himself. Having traveled about eight or ten miles, we found ourselves at Bogimovo, a magnificent, somewhat run-down estate that boasted a huge stone manor, linden-lined alleys, a charming river, several ponds, and a watermill. The rooms inside the house were so spacious that our voices echoed. The living room had columns and the reception hall had a gallery for musicians. Anton was so enchanted with Bogimovo that he decided we should move there.

The estate already had summer residents. V. A. Vagner, who later became a well-known professor of zoology, was living there with his wife and aunt, along with the artist A. A. Kiseliov and his family. Kiseliov had two sweet-natured teenagers who would entertain Anton with their stage adaptations of his stories.

Anton lived in a huge, columned room that had once been the drawing room. It held an enormous couch big enough to seat a dozen people, which is where Anton slept. When a thunderstorm swept through the estate, the lightning lit up the large windows of the drawing hall in a thrilling display. Every morning, Anton and I would rise at dawn; as soon as he had had his coffee, Anton would sit down to work at the windowsill, which he preferred to the desk. Periodically, he would look up and take in the view of the park and the horizon behind it. He was writing his story "The Duel"[4] and sorting through his materials from the trip to Sakhalin. He usually worked without a break until eleven o'clock, and would then go mushroom-picking or fishing. At one, we would all have lunch. Anton would start working again at about three and continue until the evening.

We would play games in the evening while Anton and the zoologist debated then-fashionable topics like degeneracy, survival of the fittest, natural selection, and others. Interestingly, these topics all became part of Von Koren's philosophy in "The Duel." After his experiences in Sakhalin, Anton believed that the power of a man's spirit and education could always overcome genetic mental defects. Vagner asserted that nature did not joke around—once there were signs of degeneration, that was it, there was no return. Anton argued that no matter how irreversible degeneration may seem to be, it could always be overcome through personal will and education.

Anton organized roulette for the evening entertainment as well. He wrote to Suvorin: "We now have our own roulette wheel. The stake is a kopeck and the profit is entirely invested in the joint business of picnicking. I am the banker" (May 27, four o'clock in the morning). Suvorin and even Natalia Lintvariova both paid visits to Anton, but unfortunately our most-desired guest, Lika the Beautiful, was not able to return, which we all found very disappointing.

The mongoose and the palm cat had accompanied us to Bogimovo, and that July the mongoose treated us to a first-class show. A large group of us were seated under a linden tree in the park when a three-foot snake suddenly slithered out of the bushes. The adults were horrified, while the Kiseliov children quickly jumped to their feet. "Bring the mongoose here! Quickly!" Anton cried, and I fetched the animal and set him on the ground. As soon as he saw the snake, he inflated himself into a round ball and froze. Sensing an unfamiliar enemy, the snake coiled up and lifted its head. They silently squared off, almost hypnotized. Suddenly, the mongoose leaped onto the snake, grabbed its head with his teeth, chomped down, and dragged the body into the grass.

It was becoming more and more difficult to live with these creatures. The mongoose escaped and got lost; and we had almost forgotten about him when somebody found him in a stone quarry about five miles away. The mongoose was still fat and healthy and went willingly into the hands of the man who found him. Our patience lasted until the winter back in Moscow, at which point Anton gave up and wrote a letter to the zoo, asking them to accept our animals as a gift from him. I remember that it was a biting cold day when a young man in gold-rimmed spectacles arrived to pick them up. From then on, the mongoose and the palm cat were attractions at the Moscow Zoo. My sister Maria Pavlovna visited them there more than once.

IX

MELIKHOVO

WHILE WE WERE AWAY THAT SUMMER, MY BROTHER started thinking about buying his own property again. He had twice gone back to Gogol's towns in Poltava province and had once almost made a deal in Sorochintsy, near Mirgorod. But after he spent the summer in Bogimovo he decided that what he really wanted was a country estate, and so in the winter of 1892 Anton finally became a landowner.

The newspaper had advertised an estate for sale near the Lopasnia station on the Moscow-Kursk railroad so my sister and I went to take a look. It's not a good idea to buy property in the winter when the land is covered in snow and the important features are barely visible, but we were inexperienced buyers, and in a rush because Anton had been threatening to go abroad again if we couldn't find an estate quickly. So we had to act fast.

The estate was about eight miles from the railway station but we did not know who to ask about the road conditions. We took a sled that followed an almost straight line from the station to the estate, gliding in a well-used sled track. The coachman was not a reliable source of information either, since he drove prospective buyers to see the estate and considered it his duty to praise the place.

When we arrived, we saw that all the buildings had been freshly painted in bright colors and had green and red roofs. The colorful estate stood out handsomely against the white backdrop of the snow. We were looking for a place in good enough shape that we could move in immediately, and this one appeared to meet that requirement at least. As for the condition of the woods—whether the trees were still standing or just stumps—we had no way of knowing. To be honest, though, we were so trusting that it didn't even occur to us to worry. We saw other structures around the main house, but did not think to ask whether they belonged to this property or a neighboring one. We were only worried about one thing: the estate's proximity to the village, which was just on the other side of the iron fence. The estate was called Melikhovo and was located in the Serpukhov district of Moscow province.

When we returned home, we related what we had seen to Anton and he decided to buy Melikhovo. The estate consisted of 575 acres with a house, forest, farmland, and meadows, and Anton called it "The Grand Duchy." It essentially cost him only 5,000 rubles in cash. The agreed-on price was 13,000 rubles, but the 8,000 ruble balance was to be paid to the seller in installments over the next ten years. My brother paid the money and bought the estate

sight unseen. However, before the first installment payment even came due, the former owner sent a letter im-
ploring Anton to pay off the 8,000-ruble debt right away in
exchange for a reduction in the balance owed.

I mortgaged Melikhovo to the Moscow Agricultural
Bank, where it was appraised at 21,300 rubles, essentially
forty percent more than its actual worth. But I only borrowed the 7,300 rubles needed to pay off the outstanding
debt to the seller. After that Anton no longer owed him
anything and we dealt exclusively with the bank, paying just
300 rubles a year. What kind of apartment could we rent in
Moscow for 300 rubles a year?

Anton moved in as soon as the formalities were completed. Getting around the property turned out to be a
challenge because the outbuildings were inconveniently located and there were a lot of fences, not to mention the
fact that everything was covered with snow and it was impossible to tell what was yours and what belonged to the
neighbors. Despite all of this, Anton liked Melikhovo right
away. He loved the beauty of the snow-covered estate and
the surprises that were revealed when it eventually melted.
He apparently owned a haystack that we had thought belonged to someone else and a whole row of lindens, which
the deep snow had kept hidden.

We began a life of dedicated hard work, improving or
removing anything that wasn't functional or that we didn't
like. We made the largest room, with big windows, into
Anton's study. We also had a living room, a dining room, my
sister's room, Anton's bedroom, Father's room, and

Mother's room. There was another pass-through guest-room with a Pushkin portrait in it that we solemnly named "The Pushkin Room." Despite the estate's shortcomings—the unpaved eight-mile road from the station and the lack of space—we welcomed many guests, so many that there was never enough room for them all. Sometimes guests had to sleep in the hallways or even on the porch.

As soon as the snow melted, we hired two brothers, Frol and Ivan, to work for us and serve as coachmen. Maria took over the vegetable and fruit gardens and Anton took over the planting and care of the trees. I took over the fields and farmland and rode my horse around the estate daily to keep tabs on everything. Father cleared the existing garden paths and made new ones and kept a property journal. He kept it diligently during the long years of "sitting in Melikhovo" without skipping a single day. After his death, we read through this journal, which turned out to be very sweet, almost childlike in its simplicity, and we found it quite interesting. It was later placed on display at the Chekhov Museum in Moscow. Here are a few of the entries that I remember:

> June 2. Klara Ivanovna arrived.
>
> June 3. Klara Ivanovna left.
>
> June 4. How onerous is the labor of the tiller.
>
> June 5. The peony is blooming.
>
> June 6. The fir trees in front of Antosha's windows have been cut.

Anton was interested in everything about the property—the planting of bulbs, the arrival of the birds after
the long winter, the sowing of clover, the mother goose and
her newly-hatched fluffy yellow goslings. Anton awoke very
early, often by four o'clock. He would have his coffee and
go straight to the garden. There, he would carefully exam-
ine each fruit tree and bush, either trimming it or just
squatting by the trunk and observing it carefully. We had
more land than we needed and we had to plant our crops
across the estate. We all worked together with very little
hired help—not more than a few domestic servants—
partly out of necessity, but also because we took pleasure in
the work. We were disappointed, however, as sometimes
Melikhovo peasants commented, "These landlords seem
so industrious! But are they the real landlords or not?"

Anton Pavlovich took a trip to Moscow and came back
with a box of popular books published by Sytin. He placed
them in the servants' room and every night Frol, who was
a bit of a wiseguy, would gather the servants around him
and read the books aloud. *The Captain's Daughter* by
Pushkin and *Ammalat-Bek* by Marlinsky delighted the
housemaids Masha and Anyuta and made our old cook
Marivshka Dorimedontovna[1] cry.

Because our family woke up with the sun, our lunch
would also be early, around noon. Anton Pavlovich purchased
a bell and had it fastened to a tall post in the middle of the
estate where Frol or someone else was to ring it twelve
times precisely at noon. Upon hearing the bell, everyone

within a four-mile radius would stop working and sit down to lunch.

After a few hours of writing, Anton would come to the dining room around eleven and look at the clock meaningfully. Catching this, Mother would immediately stand up from her sewing machine and begin fussing. "Ah, my-my, Antosha is hungry!" she would say and pull the cord that ran to the kitchen outbuilding. The kitchen bell would ring and Anyuta or Masha would hurry in and start the preparations for lunch. "Quickly, quickly!" Mother would say, and within minutes the table would be ready. What an idyllic picture it was! The table would be covered with homemade appetizers prepared by our loving Mother. One such lavish table of ours was immortalized in a poem by our friend T. L. Shchepkina-Kupernik. The places at the table would be filled with the five regular members of the family and an array of guests.

After lunch, Anton would usually go to his bedroom, lock himself in, and mull over his plots—if Morpheus did not interrupt him, that is. We would all go back to work from three in the afternoon until seven in the evening. With the blood of land-tilling peasants running through our veins, our family adapted well to the farming life. Suppertime was by far the merriest time at Melikhovo. The whole family would rest and relax at the table, worn out from the long day's work. Anton, as only he could, would lead the most inspiring conversations, especially when Lika the Beautiful was around. At ten o'clock, we would all go to sleep. The lights would be extinguished and the house would grow quiet. Only the sounds of our Father's soft singing and chanting could be heard.

Although this description sounds idyllic, things were not always perfect. First of all, we were all awfully tired all the time. Being inexperienced, we had thrown ourselves into farming with such ardor that we were utterly exhausted by evening, hardly able to drag our feet to bed. I would go into the fields every day at about three o'clock in the morning, before the sun even rose, and till the land with my own hands. We were so tired that when a huge fire destroyed our neighbor's manor we did not even wake up. The house stood right next to our estate, but no one in our house heard the attempts to put it out or even the alarm bell ringing from the tower. By morning, all that was left of our neighbor's house were ashes. We asked ourselves, "Where did the Kuvshinnikov house go?" and could only look at each other, dumbfounded.

Soon after Anton Pavlovich arrived, word spread that he was a doctor and people began coming to see him for help, or carting someone in for him to see, or taking him far away to see someone else who was bedridden. Early in the morning, women and children would gather in front of the house waiting for medical assistance. He would come out, listen to their complaints, and never let anybody leave without medicine. His "medical assistant" was our sister Maria Pavlovna. We maintained a complete pharmacy at our own expense. I dried various powders, prepared emulsions, and stirred ointments. More than once, peasants, mistaking me for the pharmacist, tried to slip a five-kopeck coin into my hand—one sexton even tried to give me a twenty-kopeck coin. They were all sincerely surprised when I wouldn't accept the money.

Once in a while Anton was even awoken in the middle of the night. I remember once—it was in the dead of night—some travelers had picked up a man lying in the road who had been punctured by a pitchfork. The peasant was brought in and placed on the floor of the study (I was sleeping there that night), and Anton spent a long time examining his wounds and applying bandages.

The first spring in Melikhovo was cold; there was still snow on the ground at Easter. After the snow melted, the roads turned into a dreadful mess. The estate had only come with three worn-out horses. One was lame and could not leave the stable and another was replaced with a dead one of the same color while it was left in a field unattended. All of which left us with one resigned mare, which I had to ride every day until we could buy more. We called the horse Anna Petrovna, and since we had no hay nearby we had to feed her the chopped straw. Still, Anna Petrovna managed to make it to and from the station, get Anton Pavlovich to his medical appointments, haul logs, and drag the plow. I bought seven horses as soon as I had the opportunity.

Famine seemed to be looming in Russia but we weren't very worried at Melikhovo. We had transformed the entire estate in three short months and Anton had cheered up.

The house was well-stocked; we had our own livestock, carpenters had done work on the house; and we had studied agricultural books to prepare for the work that would need to be done in the spring. Maria Pavlovna's vegetable garden produced miracles; eggplants and artichokes grew abundantly in the fresh Melikhovo air. Anton even hoped that the estate might bring him 1,000 rubles in profit, but the dry spring and summer shrunk our harvest significantly. We did not let it get us down, though, because the vegetable garden was still beautiful, we had acquired a new Allgäu heifer, and N. A. Leikin had sent two wonderful puppies named Brom and Khina from Saint Petersburg.

Our second harvest of rye was nearly four times bigger than the first. We threshed it with our own threshing machine and sent it to the mill at the Davydovsky Monastery. Due to the food shortages then going on, Anton Pavlovich instructed me to sell our flour to the Melikhovo peasants and to give them a fifty-four-pound measure of flour for each thirty-six pounds they paid for. He told me not to tell anyone at the estate, not even our Mother or sister, and I kept the secret to myself. I heard that the peasants were calling me a simpleton behind my back; one must have checked the weight of his purchase when he got home and assumed I didn't know what I was doing.

Brom and Khina were dachshunds; he black and she red. Khina had such short, wrinkled legs that when she walked her belly almost brushed the ground. Every night Khina would come to Anton, put her front paws on his knees, and look into his eyes with wistful devotion. He would change the expression on his face and speak to her in an old, cracked voice saying, "Khina Markovna! Poor thing! You'd better go to the infirmary. You'd feel much better there, wouldn't you?" He would speak to the dog like that for half an hour or more, with the rest of us doubled over in laughter. Then it was Brom's turn. He, too, would put his front paws on Anton Pavlovich's knee and the entertainment would begin again. Anton would address the dog in a worried voice, "Brom Isaevich! How is it possible? The Reverend Father had a stomachache and went behind the bushes, and some bad boys snuck up behind him and shot water at him! From a syringe! How, how did you allow this to happen?" And Brom would growl with anger.

By the time our first autumn arrived, the estate had been further transformed. We had built new outbuildings and repaired the old ones, removed the unnecessary fences, planted some beautiful rosebushes and a new flowerbed, and Anton had dug a large pond in the field in front of the gate.

How interesting it was to watch the work progress! Anton Pavlovich displayed such enthusiasm while planting trees around the pond and stocking it with small carp, perch, and tench that he had brought from Moscow in a glass jar and to whom he promised to grant "constitutional rights." This pond became more like an ichthyological station or a huge aquarium than a pond. What a variety of fish it had!

There was another, smaller pond at Melikhovo as well. It was inside the park, right in front of the windows. Be-

cause it filled with water from melting snow every spring
it was not particularly clean. During our first summer in
Melikhovo, P. A. Sergeenko and Ignaty Potapenko came
for a visit. When Sergeenko spotted this little pond, which
was already beginning to grow green slime, he got undressed, waded into the water, and started splashing.
"Potapenko," he called out from the water, "why aren't you
swimming? Quickly, get undressed!" he said. "Why would
I swim in this filthy puddle?" replied Potapenko dubiously.
"Come on, try it!" insisted Sergeenko. "I don't even want
to try it! It's filthy," said Potapenko. "But in chemistry," in-
duced Sergeenko, "there is no such a thing as filth. Look at
it like a scientist!" But Potapenko was firm: "I don't want
to look at it at all!" Sergeenko pressed on, "Oh, give Anton
some joy, swim in his puddle. Do him a favor. It is so impolite of you, to visit a new landowner and not to dip in
his cesspool!"

Even before we made the new pond, we had a well dug
in Melikhovo. Anton wanted it to have a sweep to lower
the water bucket, like they use in Ukraine, but there was
not enough room for it. Instead, the well was fitted with
a big wheel, like the ones by the railway stations. The well
turned out to have quality water. Anton was very content
with this new improvement, saying, "Well, the fresh
water–supply issue in Melikhovo has now been resolved!
Ah, wouldn't it be nice to build a new manor by the pond
now? Or to move this one to another location? That
would be so good! I can only imagine how wonderful it
will be to live on Earth in two or three hundred years!"

Anton began to seriously contemplate building a new manor. Creativity came naturally to him; he planted young trees, cultivating firs and pines from seeds and tending to them as though they were newborn babies. When he talked about his dreams for the future, he reminded me of Colonel Vershinin, the character he created in *The Three Sisters.*

The winter of 1893 was severe in Melikhovo. The snow was so high that it reached up to the windows, which were about five feet above the ground; it was so high that we were able to see the hares standing up on their hind legs right in front of the windows of Anton's study. Where the snow had been cleared, the garden paths looked like deep dug-out trenches. We lived like recluses during the winter. Maria Pavlovna would leave to teach school in Moscow and the only people left at home were Anton, Father, Mother, and I. The hours would drag and we would all go to bed even earlier than in summer. Sometimes Anton would wake up after midnight and go to his desk to work, returning to bed only in the early morning. He wrote a lot that winter.

As soon as Masha returned from Moscow and visitors started coming again, our life picked up. We sang, played piano, and laughed. There was no end to the humor and fun. Our Mother always made sure that the table was filled with good food, and our Father, a mischievous look on his face, would appear with homemade liqueurs. On those nights, Melikhovo felt extraordinary, as though it possessed something unique that no other place or family could have. Anton was especially pleased when Lika the

Beautiful and Potapenko came. We would wait for them impatiently, anxiously checking the clock and counting the minutes. When we finally heard the sound of bells and the squeaking of the skids on the snow, we would all run out into the hallway and hug our dear guests without even letting them take off their coats. On such evenings, smoke would hang in the room, we would go to bed long after midnight, and Anton Pavlovich would write only in snatches. He would write for a few minutes, perhaps five or six lines, and then come out to the guests saying with a smile, "I've just scribbled about sixty kopecks worth."

Sometimes, Potapenko and Anton would sit at the desk and write together—each working on his own piece. But for every five or six of Anton's lines, Potapenko would have written half a page or more. Once I overheard this exchange:

> Anton: "Tell me please, Ignaty Nikolaevich, how do you manage to write so fast? Here, I've written only ten lines, and you've already churned out half a page!"
> Potapenko (not lifting his eyes from the paper): "There are women who cannot deliver a child for two days or more; there are others who give birth within an hour."

Potapenko's writings appeared in thick monthly journals and thin weekly magazines. He had so many financial commitments, bills, and alimony, that whatever money he earned, it was never enough. He was always in need and managed to get advances on stories that he had not even begun or were barely written. He was incomparable in the art of negotiating an advance from a publisher; no one else could do it as skillfully. He succeeded at getting large amounts out of the same editors who would give other writers only crumbs! Potapenko would joke that "the only place where [he] would not be able to get an advance is Melikhovo."

Potapenko once did Anton a big favor with his publishing house. Anton's books *In the Twilight, Gloomy People,* and a few others[2] were all published by A. S. Suvorin's company. But when Anton needed money and asked the company for it, the accounting office answered that they did not owe him anything, and claimed that Anton in fact owed the company for printing costs. Anton was so worried about it that Potapenko offered to go to the office himself and clarify the issue when he got back to Saint Petersburg. Potapenko was able to sort it out and it turned out that the company actually owed Anton over 2,000 rubles after taxes.

Around this time, Anton was suffering from a lot of stress and anxiety, which led to trouble sleeping. As soon as he started to drift off, he would wake up in terror. He said it felt like something inside of him was being ripped out "by the roots." Then he would be unable to fall back asleep for a long time. Lika and Potapenko's visits helped to relax and distract him, especially since he and Potapenko had common literary interests. Potapenko himself, it seemed, was experiencing some of the happiest days of his life—he would sing, play the violin, make jokes, and it was pure joy to be around him.

"The Valakh Legend" was a song written by Braga[3] that was very popular in those days. When Potapenko and Lika visited Melikhovo, Lika would often sit at the grand piano and sing it. It went like this:

Oh, what sounds do I hear!
They capture my heart,
As if on the wings of Zephyr,
They come down to us from the sky.

In the song, a sick girl, delirious, hears an angel singing in heaven. She asks her mother to go out on the balcony and find out where the sounds are coming from. But the mother cannot hear them; she does not understand her daughter, and the girl falls asleep again, disappointed. Potapenko played the part of the second voice on the violin and it sounded exquisite. Anton Pavlovich found this song mystical and full of beautiful romanticism. I mention it because the song had a lot to do with the genesis of his famous story "The Black Monk,"[4] as did the following conversation we once had about apparitions.

One early summer evening, we were sitting near the gate leading to the field. It was quiet and peaceful, the sky was clear and cloudless, and we were watching the huge red circle of the sun approaching the horizon. One of us—I forget who—asked, "Why is it that when the sun is setting, it is much bigger and redder than during the day?"

After a long discussion, we decided that the reason the sun appeared big and red was because it must already be below the horizon and the air was refracting the rays of the sun like a glass prism refracts the light of a candle. What we were seeing, therefore, was not the sun itself, but a mirage of the sun. Then we started discussing whether or not a mirage itself could be refracted and produce another mirage. We wondered whether right now in the universe there could be roaming mirages that reflect landscapes, or even animals and people that existed thousands of years ago. We wondered if that was perhaps what apparitions were all about . . . Of course, that type of childish babble bordered on nonsense, but we kept ourselves entertained at Melikhovo by looking for solutions to such questions.

Soon after this conversation Anton had a dream about it. As I've mentioned, we had lunch at noon in Melikhovo, and some days the entire household would take a post-lunch nap. On such days, even Khina and Brom stopped running around and fell asleep. I was sitting near the house on a bench after lunch one day when Anton suddenly ran out of the house, rubbing his forehead and eyes. We were used to his sudden interruptions from sleep, when he would be jolted out of bed and run out into the garden, still half-asleep. I thought this was one of those times and so I asked him, "What, jolted awake again?" "No," he replied. "I just had a nightmare. A black monk appeared in my dream."

This image of a black monk flying through space was so unsettling that it took him a long time to collect himself.

He talked about it until he finally wrote it down in his famous story. I have never understood why he wrote to Suvorin on January 25, 1894 (half a year after the episode took place), saying, "A monk flying through the field came to me in my dream, and I told Misha about it after waking up in the morning." It didn't happen in the morning, but at two o'clock in the afternoon, after a nap. Then again, the episode took place in the summer, he wrote the letter in the winter, and it would not be surprising if he simply forgot. Besides, the dream is the important part.

Months passed and Melikhovo changed daily. There were moments when Anton was overcome with joy. But he also suffered from hemorrhoids constantly, which hindered his work and made him irritable. In addition, his cough came back. Hearing his cough from the dining room, our anguished Mother would glance at the icon of the Mother of God, sigh deeply, and say, "Again, Antosha coughed all night long . . ."

Anton did not like to let on when he was feeling unwell. He was afraid of worrying us, or maybe he didn't want to admit it, even to himself. In any case, he wrote to Suvorin that he was willing to drink quinine and take whatever medicine was necessary, but he would not allow any doctor to listen to his lungs. Once, I saw flecks of blood in his phlegm, but when I asked him what was wrong with him, he acted embarrassed, and concerned by his oversight, he quickly washed the phlegm away, saying, "It's nothing . . . Don't say anything to Masha and Mother." To top it all off, he developed an excruciating ache in his left temple, which caused his eye to blink uncontrollably. But all these ailments would come and go, and when they were gone, our Anton Pavlovich would be merry, work hard, and forget his recent pain.

Many local property owners, even complete strangers, began visiting Anton Pavlovich because Melikhovo was conveniently located near the big road between Lopasnia and Kashira. The summer of 1893 was especially busy, and the house was packed with visitors. There were people sleeping on couches, several in each room, and someone even slept in the hallway. Writers, young female admirers of Anton's talent, members of the district council, local doctors, and distant relatives all passed through Melikhovo in a kaleidoscopic array. Anton was at the center of all of it—he was sought-after, interviewed, and had people hanging on his every word.

We also had some very rude visitors. Hunters would occasionally show up and barge into the house with their dogs, wishing to hunt in our woods. One woman, whose head Anton compared to the head of a double bass, came and unabashedly occupied an entire room for several weeks. When someone from the family politely suggested that it was time for her to be on her way, she snapped, "I am here visiting Anton Pavlovich, not you." One neighbor in particular used to come by very often and would irritate us all with his lies. Characteristically, he would start every sentence with "Believe it or not, it's up to you . . ."

M. O. Menshikov,[5] a writer of political essays, also came to visit during this period. He was the principal writer for the magazine *The Week,* and his pieces about the possibility of happiness on earth were especially popular with readers. Menshikov had clearly been influenced by Tolstoy's philosophy and called for a life dictated by conscience and a return to nature. Menshikov had been a naval officer, so we were expecting a man in military dress. But when he actually arrived, we saw before us a man whose appearance anticipated Anton's "Man in a Case."[6] Menshikov was wearing large galoshes and a thick, padded overcoat with an upturned collar, and carrying a huge umbrella, even though it was summer and the weather was dry. He had plump, rosy cheeks and a short, thin, blondish beard. He looked more like a sexton or a reader of scripture than a writer. His articles were frankly more interesting than he was, and we breathed a sigh of relief when he finally left.

Later, when I was living in Saint Petersburg, I think it was in 1902, Menshikov showed up at my place out of the blue and spent the entire evening with me in near silence. I did not know what to talk about. Suddenly, the purpose of his visit became clear: he hinted that he would like to work for *New Time,* and asked that I pull some strings for him, as he knew that we were close to Suvorin. I could not make him any promises but he must have found another way in, because *New Time* soon began printing his "Letters to Neighbor." The articles were markedly different from his earlier writings in *The Week.* He eventually became one of the main contributors to *New Time,* and I heard that they paid him well and treated him very favorably.

Let me get back to Melikhovo. An assistant district police officer once told me in confidence, "We have been ordered to monitor your brother Anton in secret." Soon after, a young man claiming to be a doctor but dressed in a military uniform knocked on Anton's door. He started pontificating about politics, trying to ferret out Anton's political views. Then he complained about how his father had been a policeman, and how that fact had been the bane of his existence. Finally, he switched to thorny social subjects and it became obvious that he was there undercover. I was present for this conversation and to watch this man try so hard to wring some kind of political confession out of Anton was at once unpleasant and preposterous.

Among his circle of close friends, Anton Pavlovich was completely uninhibited and full of contagious good spirits. Every once in a while he would go for a ride, either around his "duchy" or to the Davydov Hermitage. He would hook his horse up to a one-seat carriage and Lika or Natasha Lintvariova would perch behind him, holding on to his belt. In his white military jacket and a uniform belt, Anton would pretend to be a cavalryman. On these rides, another carriage packed with guests would often be following behind.

The flutist A. I. Ivanenko, a very close friend of our family, lived with us in Melikhovo for a period, as did the artist O. E. Braz,[7] who spent a whole month at work on the portrait of Anton commissioned by the Tretiakov Gallery. Local public figures dropped in as well. Some of Anton's favorites were I. G. Vitte, the district physician of the Serpukhov hospital, and P. I. Kurkin, a very personable health inspector who subsequently became a well-known scholar who made a significant contribution to medical literature. Anton Pavlovich loved him very much and corresponded with him from abroad and from Yalta. At Anton's request Dr. Kurkin made a real diagram that the Moscow Art Theater used in their production of *Uncle Vanya*. It was a diagram of Serpukhov district and Dr. Astrov (played by Stanislavsky) showed it to Elena Andreevna. He was a true physician and scientist. When I visited him, I was amazed to see that the walls of his apartment were entirely covered with various patients' diagrams and charts. The diagrams could teach one everything there was to know about the health of the residents of Serpukhov.

Vitte was a very talented administrator and a bold surgeon. His hospital, which he had taken an active part in building, was considered one of the best in the country. The very hospitable Ivan Germanovich would host Anton in his apartment when he came to Serpukhov on medical business. Vitte was also passionate about planting and growing flowers; his little garden at the hospital boasted several exotic flowers from tropical climates. At the end of his life, when he lost his sight, the poor man had to leave his beloved creation behind and move to Crimea. In a letter, Anton told me, "Write to him, he'll be pleased." But Ivan Germanovich passed away soon thereafter.

Eventually, a certain gloom descended on Melikhovo that could not be dispelled, no matter how many visitors we had. Lika the Beautiful left unexpectedly for Paris and Potapenko followed her. It felt like a death, as if something precious was suddenly gone forever. We all felt twenty years older and lost interest in the things that had once seemed so captivating.

We had to keep expanding to accommodate the constant influx of guests. Anton had thought about building a separate farmstead near the recently dug-out pond or further away on another strip of land, but this never came to fruition. Instead construction started within the estate itself. We dismantled and moved some of the outbuildings to other locations and had new structures built. We erected new pens and stables and next to them a house with a well and a wattle fence like they have in Ukraine. Then came a new bathhouse, a granary, and finally Anton's dream, a separate outbuilding. It was a tiny two-story house consisting of two small rooms, with just enough space for a bed in one and a writing desk in the other. It was initially intended for guests only, but Anton Pavlovich later moved in there himself. It was where he wrote *The Seagull*. Berry bushes surrounded the guesthouse, and the path to it led through the apple orchard. It was immensely pleasant to stay there in the spring when the apples and cherries were blooming, but in winter, the snow would be so high that man-size tunnel had to be dug.

The news that Anton Pavlovich had left Moscow to settle permanently in Melikhovo inevitably led local officials to try to get him involved in the town. This resulted in Anton (and me) being elected to the local health commission. Anton got involved in public projects, helped to build schools (our sister Maria Pavlovna also lent a hand there) and a road, and supervised preparations for cholera epi-

demics. Soon nothing, not even the smallest public undertaking, happened without his participation. He had become, in this respect, very much like our Uncle Mitrofan
Egorovich.

Official papers or a summons for public service would
always be delivered by the same local official. A highly unusual man, he had been "delivering things" for thirty years,
and everyone ordered him around—the police, the justice
department, the revenue officer, the council administration, and just about everybody else. He had been running
their errands uncomplainingly for years like a lamb, despite
the fact that these errands were often of a personal rather
than official nature. He seemed to take it all in stride, as
though he'd completely accepted the inevitability of such
work. Anton depicted him in "On Official Business"[8] and in
The Three Sisters.

X

THE FINAL
YEARS

IN THE SPRING OF 1892, THE PRESS STARTED PRINTING
concerns about the grain supply in Russia. People were
worried that grain stocks were low because crops had
failed the previous year. There was concern that the next
agricultural year might not produce much of a harvest and
a severe drought that spring and summer seemed to jus-
tify these concerns. Many localities across the countryside were hit by famine, but to avoid a public outcry, the
government only referred to them as "affected by a bad
harvest."

The famine was not felt at all in Moscow and Saint Petersburg, where a loaf of white bread still cost five kopecks
and there were no shortages. The feeling in the cities was
that the famine was somewhere "out there." The pastor of
the Dutch church in Saint Petersburg organized a distri-
bution of free imported grain to the famine-stricken. The

people who brought it to Russia were treated with champagne, invited to restaurants, and honored in speeches. The intensive famine relief undertaken by private citizens and companies stood in stark contrast to the government's practically nonexistent assistance.

Anton did not shirk from his public duty; he began collecting donations and taking part in literary almanacs whose proceeds went to famine relief. The Nizhegorodsky and Voronezhsky provinces were particularly hard hit. The lieutenant E. P. Egorov, Anton's acquaintance from the Voskresensk days, was now a supervisor in the local administration there and was known as an idealist, so Anton got in touch with him, organized a charitable campaign to collect donations, and in spite of the severe winter weather, traveled to Nizhegorodsky province himself. He actually lost his way during a snowstorm and almost froze to death, but in the end, he and Egorov were able to procure workhorses for the peasants, whose survival depended on them.

Anton next went to try to help Voronezh province, this time accompanied by Suvorin. But that trip was unsuccessful. Anton found traveling with Suvorin constrictive, and he was also very upset about suppression of the provincial press. The only publication was the *Provincial Register*, and it was not independent. The lieutenant governor practically edited it himself. As in Nizhny Novgorod, he was invited to ceremonial dinners as a famous writer, but he felt that listening to speeches about famine over dinner while the rest of the province was suffering was hypocritical. As he later told me, he wanted to be involved in real action, and he threw his efforts into preventing an impending cholera epidemic.

Cholera had already swept through the southern part of Russia and was creeping closer to Moscow daily, spreading quickly because the famine had already sapped people of their strength. Urgent measures were called for; in Serpukhov, the work began in earnest, and doctors and students alike were enlisted to help. However the district's sectors were quite large, and not all the local governments were fully prepared. Anton Pavlovich was asked to take over a sector as a physician and member of the health commission, which he immediately agreed to do, without pay.

Anton's work was hard, and the local government had no money for supplies. The only quarantine facility in his sector was a cloth tent; he didn't even have a field barracks. He had to drive around the district begging local manufacturers to lend assistance in the fight against cholera. His letters to Suvorin show how poorly he was received, even by important people, whom one would have expected to be the first to help. He described his visits to Countess Orlova-Davydova and to the archimandrite of the Davydov Hermitage, who wouldn't spare any of the famous monastery's millions. He did find some generous souls who granted his requests, allowing their facilities to be used as barracks and providing equipment.

Anton Pavlovich's hard work eventually paid off and he was able to establish a network of facilities that spanned the entire twenty-five village region. Despite practically living in his coach for several months to accomplish all this, he also managed to see regular patients and continue writing. He would return home worn out, yet he would still make jokes and carry on his conversations with Khina the dog. I, too, was appointed medical guardian of a large and densely populated settlement at that time.

Thanks to his preparatory work for the cholera epidemic and his familiarity with local government representatives, Anton was elected to be a member of the local Serpukhov council. He began attending meetings and actively reviewed the many issues facing the council. He was particularly interested in the issues of public health and public education. He felt useless when it came to estimates, budgets, and petitions to the upper levels of government, but was acutely interested in the construction of new roads, hospitals, and schools—the projects with which he could most make a difference in the lives of the poor. He oversaw a variety of initiatives, from building a fire shed to erecting, at the peasants' request, a belfry with a mirror cross that shone like a beacon.

After undertaking his public service, Anton Pavlovich traveled to Yasnaya Poliana to meet Leo Nikolaevich Tolstoy in 1896. He did not want to have any escorts, or as he called them, "middlemen." Instead, he went to Yasnaya Poliana by himself. He had known for some time that Tolstoy wanted to meet him, and common friends had tried to get Anton to visit him, but he had always declined.[1]

✑   ✑

ANTON Pavlovich loved mushroom-picking, and every morning he made the rounds of his favorite places, Khina and Brom following regally behind him, and came home with handfuls of mushrooms. Jules Legras, a professor and writer from the University of Bordeaux, came to Melikhovo to visit Chekhov and arrived during one of these morning rituals. This is how he described his first meeting with Anton Pavlovich in his book *Au pays russe*:

> With a slow gait, he comes out to meet me accompanied by two ceremonious and funny dachshunds. He is slightly over thirty. He is tall, slender, with a big forehead and long hair, which he throws back with an automatic movement of his hand . . . When he talks, he is a bit cold, but without pretense. He is probably trying to figure out with whom he is dealing, sensing that he is being summed up at the same time. The tension soon dissipates, however. We start talking about how the French do not know Russians well, and vice versa, and the conversation warms up. "Why don't we go mushroom-picking?" he suddenly offers. In the quadrangle of birch trees, bent down to the ground, busy collecting *les petits rouges,* we continue our serious discussion.[2]

Legras visited us in Melikhovo more than once. He had blond hair and a typical French profile. He would drink *kvass*[3] with much gusto and hunt in our woods with even more. He loved hunting there because nobody would accuse him of poaching like they would in France. He enjoyed the feeling of freedom—so rare for a Frenchman—when he was with us. After a hunt, he would drink a shot of vodka, and then eat with great appetite. "Eat, eat, Yuly Antonovich," Anton Pavlovich would tell him. "This is *chien rôti* [roasted dog]."

Jules Legras went to inspect the Ob-Yenisei Canal in Siberia. He wrote a report about it and learned to speak Russian well, and rather quickly. When he was leaving, I asked him to pass my regards to Lika Mizinova, who was living in Paris. He later informed me that he had called on this "beautiful girl" and relayed my message.

Once Anton returned from Yasnaya Poliana to Melikhovo, he took up gardening enthusiastically. But he was also noticeably changed; we could see that he had aged, grown haggard, and that his skin had yellowed. We could also see that he was undergoing a transformation, at once internal and transcendental. I remember well how evident these changes seemed to me after a month's separation. Anton no longer showed the interest he once had in hearing my stories and anecdotes of provincial life. It was obvious that he understood the seriousness of his illness, but he still never complained and continued to hide it, even from the doctors.

Even though Anton did not enjoy my impressions as much, he still took note of a few of them. I brought him a few details from the remote town of Uglich for his story

"The Murder,"[4] and "The Wife"[5] came about after an acquaintance in Yaroslavl had shared some personal stories
with me.

Speaking of Yaroslavl, there were two curious events
that interested Anton, which I was able to attend—the
150th anniversary of Russian theater and the 50th birthday
of the poet L. N. Trefolev.[6]

Appropriately, as the city of Yaroslavl was known as
the cradle of Russian theater, the 150th anniversary festivities were taking place at the local playhouse, which was
the oldest theater in the country. Many reporters and writers from Saint Petersburg and Moscow came to town for
it, allowing me to renew some of my old contacts. The
most important event, however, was the Alexandrinsky
Theater Company's all-star performance of *The Inspector General,* starring the incomparable Davydov, Savina,
and Varlamov.[7] It was the best production of the play I
have ever seen.

The actors told me after the show that they had felt inspired by the play itself, which they had always performed
well, and by the sophistication of the audience, which came
from all over the country, but most important, by being
given the honor of performing on the stage of the very first
Russian theater on such an important day for thespians.

The Trefolev jubilee also took place in the Yaroslavl
Theater. A modest and rather inconspicuous man, Trefolev
lived in Yaroslavl, where he supported himself by working
as a clerk in the local Demidov Lyceum. He composed his
own poems and translated the Polish poet Syrokomla. His

most popular poem was "Kamarinsky Peasant," which became famous as the folk song "Along the street Varvarinskaya walked Kasian, a peasant from Kamarinsky."

Some local figure had the bright idea to make a festive occasion out of Trefolev's fiftieth birthday. They booked the theater for a night and placed a huge table covered with a piece of green cloth on the stage. Some local press and officials were then seated at the table. Finally, they sent for poor, unsuspecting Trefolev, who was brought in and given a prominent place onstage.

There he sat, old, bald, and looking like a plucked chicken. He obviously felt out of place and didn't know what to do with his hands. Later I found out that he had not even been told the evening's agenda. Still, there was an endless procession of speeches along the lines of, "Leonid Nikolaevich! Your semi-centennial activity has been so fruitful and enriching . . ." The band played flourishes, the choir sang *Glory!,* and the wretched poet only bowed and bowed.

As I mentioned, Anton wrote *The Seagull* in the small guesthouse at Melikhovo. He gave the play to the Alexandrinsky Theater in Saint Petersburg and went along to oversee its production. Soon thereafter, he wrote a bitter letter to our sister, saying that everybody around him was mean, small-minded, insincere, and that he was unhappy with the show. On the day of the first performance, Maria went to join Anton in Saint Petersburg. As she told me later, he was gloomy and depressed when he met her at the station, claiming that the actors did not understand the play, they had not learned their lines, and they did not have any interest in listening to him.

The Seagull was produced for a benefit performance for the comic actress Levkeeva,[8] which meant that the audience was expecting a comical play. As Masha told me at home later, the audience was loud and unruly. Just as had happened on the opening night of *Ivanov,* the Alexandrinsky Theater broke into chaos during *The Seagull.*

Anton disappeared from the theater after that. People looked all over for him, they even used a telephone, but he could not be found. An exhausted Masha arrived at A. S. Suvorin's house around one in the morning, still looking for Anton. But no one there knew his whereabouts either. Later, Anton sent me a postcard with the line, "The play plopped and flopped." He returned to Melikhovo without saying good-bye to anyone in Saint Petersburg.

ANTON loved books. He collected them assiduously, often bringing entire boxes home from Moscow so that over time, he established a sizable library at Melikhovo. In 1896, he donated his entire collection, including those autographed for him by their authors, to the public library in Taganrog. The city hired a member of the Academy of

Science, architect F. O. Shekhtel, to design a new building to house the library, and it eventually became a great cultural institution bearing Anton's name.

We had known Shekhtel for at least thirty-five years. He was the son of a cook from Saratov and came to Moscow in 1875 to attend the College of Painting, Sculpture, and Architecture, where he and my brother Nikolay began a friendship that lasted until Nikolay's death.

Shekhtel began calling on us frequently in 1877, when he was still a very young architecture student. We were particularly poor at the time, and as soon as he heard our Mother complain that she was out of firewood, he and his friend Helius would bring a supply. In reality, they were simply stealing logs from somebody else's stack and carrying them to us.

Shekhtel was inventive and affable, two traits which helped him advance far beyond his classmates. In 1883, his drawings were used to create "The Beautiful Spring," the grand procession held in Khodynsky Field during Alexander III's coronation festivities. From there, his popularity only grew; he created fantastic spectacles in the Hermitage Garden and in Theater Square for the famous Lentovsky.[9] His set designs for the shows *The Journey to the Moon* and *Little Hen, Golden Eggs* amazed the audience with their spectacular special effects.

He also designed a great number of buildings in Moscow and the provinces, including the Upper Bazaar and the Moscow Art Theater, for which he was elected to the Academy. Shekhtel grew very close to Anton Pavlovich after Nikolay's death, considering him to be his best friend.

      ❦   ❧

ANTON Pavlovich took an active part in the 1896 Russian census. Having conducted his own independent census of Sakhalin Island in 1890, he knew it would bring him into more contact with the people. He had always been generous with his medical expertise and was regarded as a good neighbor, but his work on the census brought him even closer to the surrounding peasants.

Anton was also involved in the plans for a Popular Club in Moscow. At that time, Russia did not have any of the social clubs common to other countries; the masses spent their free time drinking vodka in filthy inns. Anton envisioned a multifunctional public facility, built and designed by F. O. Shekhtel with capital from a joint-stock company, which would include a library, reading rooms, lecture halls, museums, and theaters. However, Anton was unable to realize this project "due to circumstances beyond his control."

In March 1897, Anton fell seriously ill. Without warning, he left Melikhovo for Moscow to meet Suvorin. They had just sat down to dinner at the Hermitage when blood started pouring out of Anton's mouth. Despite immediate medical attention, the bleeding did not stop for hours.

Only much later did our family learn what had happened that night and in the days that followed. The publication of

Suvorin's diary revealed that Anton lay in bed for two whole days. He was in Suvorin's room in the Slaviansky Bazaar hotel, where he was undoubtedly well cared for. After this episode, Anton Pavlovich was officially diagnosed with tuberculosis. According to the doctors, his health depended on his escaping the wet northern spring.

After the hospital, Anton returned to Melikhovo only briefly to prepare for his move. Although Anton always referred to his seven years in Melikhovo as his "sedentary life in Melikhovo," those years had impacted the scope and subject of his writing, which even he admitted. Stories like "Peasants" and "In the Ravine"[10] are permeated with images and characters from Melikhovo.

In search of better climates, Anton headed first to Biarritz. Encountering bad weather there, he moved on to Nice. In Nice, he settled in the Pension Russe on Gounod Street. It seems that he liked it there. He enjoyed the warmth of the climate and the politeness of the locals. He claimed that his bed was "like Cleopatra's," and people like Professor M. M. Kovalevsky, V. M. Sobolevsky, V. I. Nemirovich-Danchenko, and the artist V. I. Yakobi formed his social circle there.[11]

His expatriate friends I. N. Potapenko and A. I. Sumbatov-Yuzhin also came to Nice, and once in a while Anton Pavlovich would accompany them to Monte Carlo to play roulette. From Nice, Anton was planning to travel to Africa, but his intended traveling companion, Professor M. M. Kovalevsky, fell sick and the trip had to be cancelled.

Anton also thought about going to Corsica, but did not follow through with that either.

Anton became ill again with a high fever and acute pe-
riostitis, a chronic inflammation of the joints. Feeling dejected, he began thinking that living in Nice was just
"amoral." He couldn't take the involuntary idleness any-
more; he missed the snow and the countryside, and felt
drawn back to Russia.

Anton spent March of 1898 in Paris, where he met the
famous sculptor Mark Antokolsky.[12] Thanks to this connection, two of Antokolsky's works are now in Taganrog:
the statue of Peter the Great and the valuable composition
Last Breath.

In May, Anton finally returned to Melikhovo. His arrival brought the place back to life and visitors began arriving en masse. Anton, however, no longer joked the way
he used to; he was very pensive and rarely spoke, probably
to avoid coughing. As before, he took care of the roses and
trimmed the bushes. Our sister was involved in trying to
build a school in Melikhovo, and he appeared interested in
the project. But "the happy days in fair Aranjuez were past
and gone."[13] As Anton wrote in *Ivanov,* "Flowers still bloom
every spring, but there is no joy."[14]

Anton remained at Melikhovo until September 14. The
rains began early that year and, sensing autumn in the air,
he left for Yalta. His plan was to spend the fall there and
then go to Moscow for the opening of *The Seagull* at the
Art Theater.[15] It turned out to be a good choice; he felt quite

well throughout Yalta's temperate fall and winter. In October, though, our family suffered another sad blow. Trying to lift a heavy box filled with books off the floor in Melikhovo, our Father suffered a hernia. He was taken to Moscow for medical treatment, but the difficult trip only worsened his condition. The doctors decided to operate, and Father did not survive the surgery.

We buried him in the Novodevichy Monastery and, full of grief, Mother, Masha, and I returned to Melikhovo. Father was buried; Anton was in Yalta; Lika the Beautiful was in Paris; our friend and tenant A. I. Ivanenko had moved back to Ukraine. I walked through the empty rooms—our Melikhovo felt so deserted.

Soon after, Anton informed Masha that he had purchased a parcel of land where he was planning to build a winter house. The parcel was on the outskirts of Yalta, in a place called Autka next to a Tatar cemetery. When Anton took our sister to see his new purchase, her first impression of the overgrown, vine-filled plot was a poor one. Usatov, a former opera singer who lived in Yalta and worked for the municipality, told me that the land had been "foisted" on the impractical Anton Pavlovich. For the first three years they had to use rainwater for washing and then recycle it to irrigate the garden, as neither the water nor sanitation systems reached the property.

Anton borrowed 10,000 rubles using the future house as collateral, and managed to start construction right away. Architect L. N. Shapovalov created an excellent design for this once-neglected lot. Each stone and tree there was a testament to Anton Pavlovich and Masha's creativity. Anton spent entire days on the construction site. While the builders were working with stone and lime, Anton planted trees with the precision of a surgeon, following the growth of each new sprout like an adoring father.

But the house was still not ready by the severe winter of 1899. Anton felt exhausted by the cold, the snow, the strong winds from the sea, and the complete absence of like-minded people. He began to feel miserable. My sister told me that Anton longed for the north. He began to imagine that if he moved back to Moscow—where everything was so exciting and where he could see his plays win acclaim at the Art Theater—it would be better for his health than staying in Yalta. Yet, however unwillingly, he had to accept that Yalta was now his home.

Anton's new life quickly began making demands on him. He was elected to the board of trustees of a women's school. He also had consumptive patients writing to him from all over Russia asking him to help them come to Yalta. Anton Pavlovich took up everybody's cause, publishing appeals in newspapers, collecting donations, and helping in whatever way he could. He even donated 500 rubles to build a school in Mukholatka, near Yalta.

By the spring, however, he was no longer able to resist the pull of the north. He traveled to Moscow on April 12— where the Art Theater put on a performance of *The Seagull* especially for him—and then to Melikhovo in May.

On August 29, 1899, Anton moved into his new house in Yalta. After that, Melikhovo was sold and our Mother and sister joined Anton in the south. He would never again know his beloved north, as his life entered its final act.

❧

ON January 17, 1900, on his fortieth birthday, Anton was elected honorary member of the Academy of Sciences, Pushkin Section. Our family was so happy! When I came to Crimea, I remember Mariushka, our very, very old cook, who was living with Anton in Yalta, coming out of the house and telling me with much gravity, "Now our dear Anton Pavlovich is a general."

After his election, some people started calling Anton Pavlovich "Your Excellency"—some jokingly, others seriously. Even important people like the concierge of the Livonia Palace used the honorific "Excellency."

In the spring, the Art Theater came to Crimea. Anton was expected to join Stanislavsky[16] and the actors while they were playing in Sevastopol, but the weather was so bad that he never made it. He came only for Easter, when the weather warmed up. They staged *Uncle Vanya* especially for him.

From Sevastopol, the theater moved to Yalta. Chirikov, Bunin, Elpatievsky, Kuprin, and Maxim Gorky arrived to see Anton and the theater group.[17] Every day the entire company of actors, along with the writers, would gather in the Autka house and the place would come alive. It was like Melikhovo all over again, with Masha and Mother attending to the guests. Our gray-haired and affectionate Mother would reign at the head of the table, offering food and seeing to it that every guest ate well.

After the theater company left, the flow of visitors continued to overwhelm Anton Pavlovich. Guests, guests, and more guests! Strangers would show up and engage him in meaningless conversations for hours at a time, or—worse yet—sit drinking glasses of tea in complete silence. Meanwhile Anton might have been in the perfect mood to write! To escape, he would have to abandon his own desk and lock himself in the bedroom.

"I am being harassed," he wrote in one of his letters. "Harassed badly. The play is ready in my head, already fully formed, asking to be on paper, but as soon as I sit down, the door opens and in creeps a face!"[18]

Anton Pavlovich spent the autumn of 1900 in Moscow. He went abroad again in early December, but the snow and cold chased him back to Yalta in the first days of February, 1901. I was in the north during that time and did not receive any letters from either him or the family, so I do not know how he spent his time until spring. Then suddenly, in late May of 1901, I read in the papers that Anton had gotten married.[19] The wedding took place in Moscow on May 25, 1901. I did not even know who his bride was. Even my brother Ivan Pavlovich, who was in Moscow at the time and had seen Anton about an hour before the wedding ceremony, only learned about it after the fact.

His wife, Olga Leonardovna Knipper, took her husband off to drink *kumiss*[20] in Ufa province right after the ceremony. I lost touch with my brother Anton after that and never saw him again.

🙰   🙰

THREE years later, on July 3, 1904, I went to Yalta to visit my Mother and sister. Anton Pavlovich and his wife were abroad, in Badenweiler. When the steamship pulled up to the pier, I saw someone standing on the pier waving his hat at me. It was my cousin George, who worked as an agent for the Russian steamship line in Yalta and had come out onto the pier to receive the ship. He recognized me from a distance and, cupping his hands around his mouth, yelled up to me, "Anton passed away!"[21]

Suddenly all the extraordinary colors of the trip, the mountains and the sea, and even beautiful Yalta lost their appeal. The news struck me like a thunderbolt. I felt like crying. I went straight to Autka. My sister and brother Ivan were in Borzhom at the time. We sent Masha an urgent telegram, but kept the news a secret from Mother. She had no idea what had happened and met me with her usual joy and tenderness.

As always, she wanted to feed me, but I could not eat. I felt uncomfortable to be keeping such important news from her, having to pretend in order to ease the blow. Masha and Ivan returned to Yalta, and a telegram from Anton's widow soon followed, informing us that his body was being transported through Saint Petersburg to Moscow. The news began appearing in the papers. I was only in Yalta for five days before I had to go back north to meet the train with Anton's body and escort it to the grave.

Masha was going to come, too. We decided to tell our Mother before we left. She grabbed her head with her hands, sat down on the steps of the stairway, and sobbed. It tore at my heart to witness her in such terrible grief. Then, she slowly quieted, and started packing to go to Moscow with us. The four of us, including Ivan, took off to the north and the Yalta house was left abandoned.

We arrived in Moscow just in time for the funeral. V. S. Miroliubov[22] picked us up at the station and drove us toward the university in his carriage. The body had already arrived from Saint Petersburg and was on its way from Nikolaevsky station to Novodevichy Monastery. Had our train been delayed, we would have missed the funeral.

An enormous crowd accompanied the coffin; traffic had been blocked and the adjacent streets roped off. No one recognized us as the family of the deceased and we were only able to join the procession along the way. A group of Moscow youth formed a huge circle to protect the procession from the thousands of followers trying to glimpse the coffin.

As the procession approached the narrow monastery gate, there was a terrifying bottleneck. Everyone was scrambling to get inside as quickly as possible. If it had not been for the Moscow students again, there might have been a real stampede. They were barely able to carry the coffin through the gate. We managed to press through the gate as the crowd pushed from behind. Finally, the entire crowd rolled into the cemetery, crushing crosses, pushing monuments, breaking fences, and trampling flowers.

Brother Anton was lowered into his grave, next to our Father. We looked at the coffin for the last time and each threw down a parting handful of earth—it made a knocking sound. Then they covered the grave and the famous author with it.

NOTES

PREFACE

1. Reprinted in 1959, 1960, 1964, 1980, and 1981.
2. Quoted in Alevtina Kuzicheva, *Chekhovy: Biografia semyi* (Artist, Rezhisser, Teatr: Moscow, 2004) p. 332.

PREFACE AND CHRONOLOGY REFERENCES

Evgeny Balabanovich, "Kniga 'Vokrug Chekhova' i eyo avtor" in Mikhail Chekhov, *Vokrug Chekhova: Vstrechi i vpechatlenia* (Moskovsky Rabochy: Moscow, 1964).

A. P. Chekhov, *Polnoe sobranie sochinenii i pisem v 30 tomakh.* (Nauka: Moscow, 1974–1983).

Alevtina Kuzicheva, *Chekhovy: Biografia semyi* (Artist, Rezhisser, Teatr: Moscow, 2004).

Donald Rayfield, *Anton Chekhov: A Life* (Northwestern University Press: Evanston, 1997).

CHAPTER I

1. Mitrofan Egorovich Chekhov (c. 1832–1894).
2. *Mama's Boy (Mamenkin synok)*, most likely a comedy by Piotr Karatygin published in 1878. *Misfortunes of a Gentle Heart (Beda ot nezhnogo serdtsa)* by Vladimir Sollogub, published in 1850.
3. Mitrofan and his wife Lyudmila had six children: Georgy (1870–1943), Olimpiada (1870–1872), Vladimir (1874–1949), Ivan (1876–1876), Alexandra (1877–1957), and Elena (1881–1922).
4. Mitrofan Egorovich's writing emulated the style of the Russian writer and romantic poet Alexander Bestuzhev-Marlinsky (1797–1837).
5. Grigory Danilevsky (1829–1890), Russian writer. His novel *New Places* was published in 1867.
6. Pavel Egorovich Chekhov (1825–1898), father.
7. Tsarskoe Selo (literally Tsars' Village) is the old name of what is now the city of Pushkin. Located fifteen miles south of Saint Petersburg, Tsarskoe Selo was a

1710 gift from Tsar Peter the Great to Marta Skavronskaya. Two years later Marta became his second wife, assuming the name of Tsarina Ekaterina.

8. Evgenia Yakovlevna Morozova (c.1831–1919), mother.

9. The name "Old Believers" refers to a group that separated from the hierarchy of the Russian Orthodox Church in 1666–1667. In a protest against church reforms introduced by Patriarch Nikon, the Old Believers continued liturgical practices that the Russian Orthodox Church had had before the implementation of the reforms; hence the name.

10. July 21 is a religious holiday in the Russian Orthodox Church celebrating the holy icon of Our Lady of Kazan.

11. Alexander Chekhov (1855–1913) died from throat cancer. Aside from son Mikhail (1891–1955), he had daughter Maria (1883–1884) and sons Nikolay (1884–after 1920) and Anton (1886–after 1921).

12. Nikolay Chekhov (1858–1889) died from consumption.

13. Ivan Pavlovich Chekhov (1861–1922); Maria Pavlovna Chekhov (1863–1957).

CHAPTER II

1. A series of criminal trials held in Saint Petersburg in 1877–1878, in which 193 people were charged with propaganda against the Russian Empire.

2. Ivan Turgenev (1818–1883), Russian writer, poet, and member of the Saint Petersburg Academy of Science.

3. Nadezhda Sigida (Malaksiano) (1862–1889) died after she took poison in protest against corporal punishment of women.

4. "Easter Eve" (*Sviatoyu nochiu*), published in 1886.

5. A Russian bat-and-ball game.

6. The play was apparently *Muscovite the Miracle Worker* (*Moskal-Charovnik*), published in 1841, by Ivan Kotliarevsky (1769–1838), a major Ukrainian poet, writer, and dramatist.

7. "Happiness" (*Schastie*), published in 1887.

8. "The Lights" (*Ogni*), published in 1888; "Fears" (*Strakhi*), published in 1886.

9. Once in school, during Greek class, Zembulatov switched the stress in the word "blessed" (makar) from the first to the second syllable, making it sound like the Russian name "Makar." (In Alevtina Kuzicheva *Vash A. Chekhov. Soglasie:* Moscow, 2000, p. 192).

10. *Without a Father* (*Bezotsovshchina*), a play written when Anton Chekhov was nineteen years old, but only discovered twenty years after his death. Produced as *Platonov.*

11. *The Chicken Didn't Sing in Vain* (*Nedarom kuritsa pela*). The name of the play is known only from a letter by Alexander Chekhov.

12. Aleksey S. Suvorin (1834–1912), Russian journalist and publisher.

CHAPTER III

1. *Three Years* (*Tri goda*), published in 1894.

2. Eastern Catholicism.

3. Nikolay Chernyshevsky (1828–1889), Russian philosopher, writer, and literary critic. His novel *What Is to Be Done?* containing revolutionary ideas, was published in 1863.

4. The author must have mixed two different events into one: the Secretary Delianov memo was issued in 1887. At that time Mikhail was a twenty-two year old university student, and no longer in danger of being expelled from school.

5. Olga Kundasova (c.1865–1943), friend

6. Frants O. Shekhtel (1859–1926), architect.

7. *Dragonfly (Strekoza)*, a weekly magazine published from 1876 to 1908.

8. The joke relies on the consonance of the words *sorter* and *sortir*. The latter, although a French verb meaning to leave (as in "*je dois sortir*"), came to be used in conversational Russian as a euphemism for "restroom."

9. Andrey Dmitriev, writer and editor, died in 1886.

10. "Ivan Matveevich," published in 1886.

CHAPTER IV

1. Alexander Kurepin (1847–1891), journalist and playwright.

2. Nikolay Kicheev (1847–1890), journalist, playwright, and translator of plays. Editor of *Alarm Clock*.

3. Maria Ermolova (1853–1928), actress.

4. Fiodor Popudoglo (1846–1883), author of short stories and plays published in Moscow and Saint Petersburg papers and magazines.

5. Mikhail (Misha) Evstigneev (1832–1885), author of more than 150 popular books. He wrote short stories, humor, parodies, poems, fairy tales, folktales, mystery novels, historical novels, and songbooks, many of which he also illustrated. His books sold up to 50,000 copies a year.

6. Ivan D. Sytin (1851–1934), publisher. A self-made man, he started as an apprentice in a Moscow bookshop, but in 1876 he opened a small printshop where he successfully printed maps of the battles during the Russian-Turkish War of 1877–1878. Later he published pictures and books based on Russian fairy tales, but also textbooks for schools and low-cost books for mass consumption. He also published the magazines *Around the World* (1891–1917), *The Spark* (1897–1916), and the newspaper *Russian Word* (1897–1917).

7. Piotr Sergeenko (1854–1930), writer, schoolmate of Anton.

8. Vladimir Giliarovsky (1853 or 1855–1935) was a writer and journalist best known for his reminiscences of life in pre-revolutionary Moscow (*Moscow and Muscovites*), which he first published in book form in 1926.

9. Liodor Palmin (1841–1891), poet and translator.

10. Ignaty Potapenko (1856–1929), writer and playwright; one of Russia's most popular writers of the 1890s.

11. In January 1899, Anton Chekhov signed a contract with the publisher Adolf Marks. According to the contract, Chekhov sold Marks all his previously published works, as well as those that would be written during the next twenty years, for 75,000 rubles.

12. Nikolay Leikin (1841–1906), writer and publisher. During his life he wrote thirty-six novels, eleven plays, and more than 10,000 short stories, essays, and

one-act plays. From 1882 to 1905 Leikin edited the magazine *Fragments,* where Anton published more than two hundred short stories.

13. Dated April 8, 1892.

14. Nikolay Teleshov (1867–1957), writer. He became well known after he traveled to Siberia in 1894 and published a series of short stories based on the trip. Later Teleshov worked as the director of the Moscow Art Theater's museum.

15. The Union of Writers of the USSR was a quasi-governmental organization that absorbed other writers' organizations in 1932 and existed until the collapse of the Soviet regime. Nominally, it was a professional union assisting its members, but in reality it was used to control and censor literature.

16. *Cape Green* (*Zelyonaya kosa*), published in 1882.

17. *The Shooting Party* (*Drama na okhote*), published in 1884.

18. *Unnecessary Victory* (*Nenuzhnaya pobeda*), published in 1882.

19. Mavr Iokai or Mór Jókai (1825–1904), a Hungarian novelist and playwright, and Friedrich von Spielhagen (1829–1911), a German novelist.

20. Nikolay Pushkariov (1841–1906), poet, journalist, and translator.

21. Nikolay Nekrasov (1821–1877), writer, publisher, and one of the most important Russian poets of the nineteenth century.

22. *Late-Blooming Flowers* (*Tsvety zapozdalye*), published in 1882.

23. Aleksey A. Ostroumov (1844–1908), physician and professor of the Moscow University.

CHAPTER V

1. Pavel Golokhvastov (sometimes spelled Golokhvostov), (1838 or 1839–1892), writer, historian, and linguist specializing in Russian folktales.

2. The Time of Troubles (1598–1613), a period of Russian history between the death of Tsar Fiodor and the establishment of the Romanov Dynasty. Occupied by the Polish-Lithuanian Commonwealth, Russia also suffered from uprisings, usurpers, and impostors.

3. Olga Golokhvastova (1840–1897), writer and dramatist. She published several novels and plays, two of which were produced by the Imperial Alexandrinsky Theater in Saint Petersburg. Both of her plays, *Evil to the Evil* (*Likhomu likhoe*) and *Call Yourself a Mushroom—Jump into the Basket* (*Nazvalsia gruzdem, polezay v kuzov*), were published in Moscow in 1881.

4. "Children" (*Detvora*), published in 1886.

5. *The Three Sisters* (*Tri sestry*), published and premiered in the Moscow Art Theater in 1901.

6. Piotr Shostakovsky (1851-1917), pianist and conductor.

7. "Two Scandals" (Dva scandala), published in 1882.

8. "Actors' Wives" (Zhiony artistov), published in 1880. "Flying Islands" (Letayushchie ostrova), published in 1883.

9. Mikhail Saltykov-Shchedrin (1826–1889), satirical writer.

10. *Otechestvennye zapiski, Vestnik Evropy,* and *Istorichesky vestnik,* respectively. All three were monthly magazines published in Saint Petersburg during the following periods: *Otechestvennye zapiski,* from 1818 to 1884 (with some interruptions); *Vestnik Evropy* from 1866 to 1918; and *Istorichesky vestnik* from 1880 to 1917.

11. "Escapee" (*Beglets*), published in 1887. "Surgery" (*Khirurgia*), published in 1884. "The Government Test" (*Ekzamen na chin*), published in 1884.

12. "A Dead Body" (*Miortvoe telo*), published in 1885. "During an Autopsy" (*Na vskrytii*), published as "On Official Business" (*Po delam sluzhby*) in 1899. "Siren" (*Sirena*), published in 1887.

13. A restaurant with musical performances, like cabaret, that originated in France but became popular in Russia in the second part of the nineteenth century. Attendance was often associated with indecency.

14. *Réminiscences des Huguenots,* a piano piece by Franz Liszt based on Giacomo Meyerbeer's 1836 opera *Les Huguenots.*

15. "The Teacher of Literature" (*Uchitel slovesnosti*), published in 1889.

16. "The Death of a Government Official" (*Smert chinovnika*), published in 1883. "Volodia," published in 1887. "The Burbot" (*Nalim*), published in 1885. "The Daughter of Albion" (*Doch Albiona*), published in 1883.

17. Boleslav Markevich (1822–1884), writer and journalist. He had conservative views and criticized even those government reforms that abolished serfdom in Russia in the 1860s. His novel *Abyss* (*Bezdna*) was not finished.

18. Alexander Dargomyzhsky (1813–1869) and Piotr Tchaikovsky (1840–1893), composers. Tommaso Salvini (1829–1915), Italian actor.

19. See Chapter I, note 10.

20. "The Witch" (*Vedma*), published in 1886. "Evil Deed" (*Nedobroe delo*), published in 1887.

21. Aleksey Pisemsky (1821-1881), writer.

22. "And happiness was so possible, so close!" (*A schastie bylo tak vozmozhno, tak blizko!*), a line from Pushkin's novel *Eugene Onegin,* and from Tchaikovsky's opera of the same name.

23. Mikhail Lermontov (1814–1841), poet, writer, and playwright. The story *Bela,* the first part of his novel *A Hero of our Time,* was published in 1839. Tchaikovsky's plan to compose an opera from Chekhov's libretto based on the story never materialized.

24. *Gloomy People* (*Khmurye lyudi*), published in 1890.

25. Dmitry Grigorovich (1822–1899), writer.

26. "The Gamekeeper" (*Eger*), published in 1885.

27. Lika Mizinova (1870–1939), a close friend of the family.

28. Isaak Levitan (1860–1900), artist, master of landscape painting.

29. *A Quarter Century Ago,* published in 1878.

30. *Moscow Bulletin* (*Moskovskie vedomosti*), a newspaper published from 1756 to 1917.

31. Sofia Kuvshinnikova (1857–1907), Russian painter.

32. "The Butterfly" (*Poprygunia*), published in 1892. This story is also known in English as "The Grasshopper."

33. Tatiana Shchepkina-Kupernik (1874–1952), writer, playwright, poet, and translator.

CHAPTER VI

1. Konstantin Pobedonostsev (1827–1907), jurist, professor of civil law, statesman, and a close adviser to the Tsar Alexander III. A conservative, he was instrumental in setting government policy in, among other things, education.

2. The name refers to the trial of Tsar Alexander II's assassins. The assassination took place on March 1, 1881.

3. From Alexander Pushkin's 1825 poem to K. (Anna Kern).

4. *The Cherry Orchard* (Vishniovy sad), premiered in 1903.

5. Aleksey Pleshcheev (1825–1893), poet, writer, and translator from English, French, and German.

6. The Petrashevsky Affair involved a gathering of intellectuals who supported political and social reform, including the emancipation of Russia's 20 million serfs. The leaders of the Petrashevsky Affair (including Fiodor Dostoevsky) were sentenced to death; they were granted reprieve a mere twenty seconds before the execution, and were sentenced instead to hard labor in Omsk (in Siberia).

7. *New Time* (*Novoe vremia*), a newspaper published between 1868 and 1917.

8. Pavel Svobodin (real name Pavel Kozienko, 1859–1892), character actor.

9. Anatoly Koni (1844–1927), jurist and writer.

10. Victor Burenin (1841–1926), journalist, poet, and dramatist.

11. *The Saint Petersburg Register* (*Sankt-Peterburgskie vedomosti*), a newspaper published from 1728 to 1917.

12. In March 1898, *New Time* published a number of articles attacking the French writer Émile Zola for his demand to reopen and reexamine the case against Dreyfus.

13. *The Story of an Unknown Man* (*Rasskaz neizvestnogo cheloveka*), published in 1892.

14. October 23, 1887.

15. Victor Alexandrov (real name Victor Krylov, 1838–1906), one of the most prolific playwrights of the period. More than thirty of his original plays and over seventy of his adaptations of foreign works were produced during his lifetime.

16. *The Bear* (*Medved*), premiered in 1888.

17. Ivan Shcheglov (real name Ivan Leontiev, 1856–1911), writer.

18. Grigory Potiomkin (1739–1791), a man of relatively modest origins who nevertheless became a prince, statesman, general field marshal, and favorite of Catherine the Great.

19. *Shchegol,* from which comes the last name Shcheglov, is the Russian word for *goldfinch.*

20. Piotr Nevezhin (1841–1919), writer and dramatist. His drama *The Second Youth* (*Vtoraya molodost*) was published and produced in 1887.

21. Glikeria Fedotova (1846–1925), Elena Leshkovskaya (1864–1925), Alexander Yuzhin (Sumbatov) (1857–1927), Konstantin Rybakov (1856–1916).

22. In Russian, to "burn down" also means to "go bankrupt."

23. Mitrofan Ivanov-Kozelsky (1850–1898), Modest Pisarev (1844–1905), Vassily Andreev-Burlak (1844–1888), Luka Nikolaevich Antropov (1841–1881), playwright.

24. Leonid Gradov-Sokolov (1845–1890), Piotr Solonin (1857–1894), Vladimir Davydov (real name Ivan Gorelov) (1849–1925), Alexandra Glama-Meshcherskaya (1859–1942), Natalia Rybchinskaya (Dmitrevskaya) (?–1920), Glafira Martynova (1861–1928), Elizaveta Krasovskaya (1822–1898).

25. Victorien Sardou (1831–1908), French playwright. Édouard Pailleron (1834–1899), French poet and dramatist. Alphonse Daudet (1840–1897), French novelist and playwright.

CHAPTER VII

1. Nikolay Chekhov (1858–1889) died from consumption.

2. Glafira Panova (1869–?) played in the Maly Theater (Moscow) from 1888 to 1895 and in the Alexandrinsky Theater (Saint Petersburg) from 1895 to 1907.

3. Alexander Lensky (real name Verviziotti) (1847–1908), actor and director. A friend of Anton from 1888 until 1892 when, after the publication of the story "The Butterfly," Lensky recognized himself in it as "the fat actor."

4. "A Dull Story" (*Skuchnaya istoriya*), published in 1889.

5. *The Wood Demon* (*Leshiy*), later reworked as *Uncle Vanya.*

6. Nikolay Solovtsov (real name Fiodorov) (1857–1902), actor, director, and entrepreneur. Maria Abramova (real name Heinrich) (1865–1892), actress and entrepreneur. During the season of 1889/1890, they ran a private theater in Moscow.

7. Elena Shavrova (1874–1937), singer and writer.

8. Maria Glebova (1840s–1919), actress and entrepreneur, wife of Nikolay Solovtsov.

9. Nikolay Roshchin-Insarov (real name Pashenny) (1861–1899), actor.

10. Nikolay Zubov (real name Popov) (1826–1890) played the role of Orlovsky in Chekhov's *Wood Demon.*

11. *The Power of Darkness* (*Vlast tmy*), play by Leo Tolstoy published in 1887 but allowed for production only in 1895.

12. *The Swan Song* (*Lebedinya pesnya*), produced on February 19, 1888 in the Korsh Theater.

13. See Chapter IV, note 12.

14. Gaston Calmette (1858–1914), French journalist, editor of *Le Figaro* from 1902 to the day he was assassinated in his office in 1914.

15. Mathilde Kschessinskaya (1872–1971), ballerina; Anastasia Vialtseva (1871–1913), actress and singer.

16. Madame Angot is the name of a then-popular character from Charles Lecocq's *opéra comique La fille de Madame Angot.* Madame Adan was a French journalist who advocated for a French-Russian alliance.

17. Nikolay Leskov (1831–1895), writer. His books include: *The Steel Flea* (1881), *Cathedral Folk* (1872), *The Sealed Angel* (1873), *Little Things from the Lives of Bishops* (1879), *Nowhere* (1864), and *At Daggers Drawn* (1870).

18. *The Proposal* (*Predlozhenie*), published in 1889.

19. *The Steppe* (*Step*), published in 1888.

20. Alexander Ostrovsky (1823–1886), playwright, member of the Saint Petersburg Academy.

21. Vladimir Korolenko (1853–1921), writer.

CHAPTER VIII

1. After a two-and-a-half month journey across Russia and Siberia, Chekhov arrived at Sakhalin Island on July 11, 1890, and sailed from it on October 13, 1890. During his three months in the penal colony he interviewed thousands of people (convicts, exiles, settlers, and government officials) to compile a cen-

sus. It wasn't until five years later that he finished organizing the materials collected on the trip and published them in the book *Sakhalin Island*.

2. March 9, 1890.
3. Published in 1890.
4. "The Duel" (*Duel*), published in 1891.

CHAPTER IX

1. Mariushka Dormidontovna [Dorimedontovna] Belenovskaya, (1826–1906), cook who lived in the Chekhov family from 1886 until she died.
2. *In the Twilight* (*V sumerkakh*), the 1887 book of short stories for which Chekhov received the Pushkin Award a year later. *Gloomy People* (*Khmurye lyudi*) was a collection of short stories published in 1890.
3. "The Valakh Legend" (originally "La Serenata" known in English as "Angel's Serenade") written by Italian composer Gaetano Braga (1829–1907).
4. "The Black Monk" (*Chiorny monakh*), published in 1893.
5. Mikhail Menshikov (1859–1919), journalist.
6. "A Man in a Case" (*Chelovek v futliare*), published in 1898.
7. Osip Braz (1872 or 1873–1936), artist.
8. "On Official Business" (*Po delam sluzhby*), published in 1899.

CHAPTER X

1. The first meeting between Anton Chekhov and Leo Tolstoy took place on August 8, 1895. In his letters to A. S. Suvorin, Chekhov wrote, "I spent at [Tolstoy's] a day and a half. My impression is wonderful. I felt as comfortable as if I were at home and my conversations with Leo Nikolaevich were effortless" (October 21, 1895). "Tolstoy's daughters are very nice. They adore their father and believe in him fanatically, and this is proof that Tolstoy is indeed a great moral force. For if he were insincere or flawed, the daughters would be the first ones to treat him with skepticism. Daughters are impossible to deceive. One may deceive a wife or a mistress—in the eyes of a loving woman, even an ass is a great philosopher—but daughters are altogether different" (October 26, 1895). Excerpted from Anton Chekhov, *The Complete Works and Letters* (Moscow: *Gosudarstvennoe izdatelstvo khudozhestvennoy literatury* [State Publisher of Fiction Literature], 1949.)
2. Published by Armand Colin et Cie, Editeurs, Paris, 1895.
3. A fermented bread drink.
4. "The Murder" (*Ubiystvo*), published in 1895.
5. "The Wife" (*Supruga*), published in 1895.
6. Leonid Trefolev (1839–1905), poet and translator.
7. Maria Savina (1854–1915), Konstantin Varlamov (1849–1915).
8. Elizaveta Levkeeva (1851–1904).
9. Mikhail Lentovsky (1843–1906), actor and entrepreneur.
10. "Peasants" (*Muzhiki*) and "In the Ravine" (*V ovrage*), published in 1897 and 1899, respectively.

11.   Maxim Kovalevsky (1851–1916), sociologist, historian, and jurist. Vassily Sobolevsky (1846–1913) economist, publisher, and editor of *Russian Register* (*Russkie vedomosti*). Vassily Nemirovich-Danchenko (1848–1936), writer and older brother of Vladimir, the founder of the Moscow Art Theater. Valery Yakobi (1834–1902), artist.

12.   Mark Antokolsky (1843–1902), sculptor.

13.   The first line from the play *Don Carlos* by Johann Schiller.

14.   Act 1, Scene 6.

15.   *The Seagull* opened in Moscow on December 17, 1898.

16.   Konstantin Stanislavsky (1863–1938), actor and director. With Vladimir Nemirovich-Danchenko he founded the Moscow Art Theater in 1898.

17.   Evgeny Chirikov (1864–1932), writer. Ivan Bunin (1870–1953), writer, winner of the Nobel Prize for Literature. Sergey Elpatievsky (1854–1933), writer. Alexander Kuprin (1870–1938), writer. Maxim Gorky (1868–1936), writer.

18.   August 18, 1900.

19.   Anton Chekhov married Olga Knipper (1868–1959), a leading actress of the Moscow Art Theater. Knipper's entire acting career was spent with the company, spanning from 1898 (she was one of the original members) until her death in 1959. Knipper played leading roles in all of Chekhov's major plays, with some of them written specifically for her.

20.   *Kumiss* is fermented camel or mare milk believed to help in the treatment of tuberculosis.

21.   Anton Chekhov died at three o'clock in the morning on July 2, 1904 in Badenweiler, Germany. In her July 4, 1904, letter to her mother, Olga Knipper described his final hours: "He fell asleep, but soon after midnight he woke up mumbling something unintelligible. He tried to remove the ice from his chest, saying that an empty heart didn't need ice. At two o'clock he told me to send for the doctor. When the doctor arrived, Anton told him, 'I am dying,' and repeated it in German, '*Ich sterbe.*' The doctor gave him a big injection of camphor and then offered him a glass of Champagne. But Anton's heart was getting weaker, and before I could even get to the other side of his bed, he had passed—without a sigh, without pain, without a sound—as if he had fallen asleep." Excerpted from *Olga Leonardovna Knipper-Chekhova: Vospomimaniai perepiska* (Moscow: Iskusstvo, 1972).

22.   Victor Miroliubov (1860–1939), opera singer (stage name Mirov) and journalist. He published *Magazine for Everybody* (*Zhurnal dlia vsekh*), in which Chekhov printed his last stories, "The Bishop" (*Arkhierey*) and "The Bride" (*Nevesta*), in 1902 and 1903, respectively.

INDEX